# CRAFT SHOW & SELL

How to build your craft business
at home, online and in the marketplace

## TORIE JAYNE

Search Press

A Quintet book
First published in the UK in 2014 by
Search Press Ltd.
Wellwood , North Farm Road
Tunbridge Wells
Kent TN2 3DR
United Kingdom
www.searchpress.com

ISBN 978-1-78221-042-9

This book was conceived, designed and produced by
Quintet Publishing Limited
4th Floor, Sheridan House
114-116 Western Road
Hove, East Sussex BN3 1DD
United Kingdom

Project Editor: Caroline Elliker
Designer: Maru Studio
Photographer: Sussie Bell
Art Director: Michael Charles
Publisher: Mark Searle

10 9 8 7 6 5 4 3 2 1

Printed in China by 1010 Printing International Ltd.

# CONTENTS

# INTRODUCTION

Y ou've always had a knack for creating charming homespun crafts, and now you've created something highly original that always gets a good reaction when you show it off to friends, family and co-workers. In short, you've got a passion for your craft, and it shows.

You've decided you want to start selling your crafts. How? Where? Unfortunately, it isn't enough just to make gorgeous crafts – you need to stand out from the crowd and get noticed. This book will give you the answers. From how to organise your space, brand yourself and your products, to how to photograph your work and market your wares, I will provide you with my firsthand knowledge as well as tips and advice from other crafters who are already highly successful in showing and selling their crafts.

We will start with the basics of setting up a craft room or space to keep you motivated, inspired and organised. I will give you tutorials on how to upcycle salvaged finds to give your craft room a personalised look. I'll teach you about inspiration and mood boards and why designers use them, so you can create your own to inspire your craft projects and pull together your very own unique brand to set you apart from the competition. I will delve into branding and show you that it's not something only large corporations do, but it is just as important for you.

Once you've built your brand, it's time to get it out into the marketplace. We will look at popular options: selling at a craft fair, with tips on setting up your stall to engage customers and get them coming back for more; selling through external marketplaces such as Etsy; and promoting your goods in person and online, including setting up a blog and using social media to the best effect.

Making the jump from hobby crafter to a branded business can seem like a daunting task, but here you will learn all the basics and hopefully be inspired to become the next big thing!

Love
Jayne

# CHAPTER 1
# GETTING STARTED

There's nothing a crafter likes better than going behind the scenes of another crafter's creative workspace. How someone organises their space or workshop can say a lot about their brand. It's the first thing you should think about when you're getting started.

- Choosing and organising a crafting workspace (page 10)
- Storage solutions (page 15)
- Creative boards (page 36)

# CHOOSING AND ORGANISING A CRAFTING WORKSPACE

Being well organised is the key to keeping your creative space tidy and inspiring. If your craft space becomes overwhelmingly cluttered, it can sap your creative energy. Dealing with a mess of tangled ribbons, loose buttons and scissors (that become invisible just when you need them) makes you lose valuable time. Over the next few pages, crafters like Emma Lamb (page 14), Helena Schaeder Söderberg from Craft & Creativity (page 22), Elyse Major from Tinkered Treasures (page 42), and I will show you how to get your craft room into shape. Whether you enjoy card making, scrapbooking, crocheting or sewing, you'll have more time for working on the things you love.

First you need to choose a location that can serve as a permanent workspace where you can keep all your supplies and materials together. Those who have an entire room to devote to creative pursuits are fortunate. Pressed for space? Even a corner of a room or a spacious cabinet can function beautifully as long as it is dedicated to making your ideas and inspirations come to life. Consider natural light sources as much as possible and try to select a tranquil place where you can dream your creative dreams.

Next, take stock of your supplies and start organising them into groups. The key to organising your craft space is to store everything in categories that make sense to you and to keep all the materials you use regularly within reach. Don't be tempted to start buying containers right away as you might end up with less-than-optimal storage solutions. If you have multiple hobbies, try organising by hobbies and keep things separate.

Once you have sorted all your supplies, you can start looking into storage options. The right containers make all the difference when it comes to storing materials, such as glass jars for easily lost items and open bins on the floor to keep ongoing projects accessible and portable. Don't limit your search to container and craft shops. Instead, get creative and find uses for items you already have or upcycle items you find at jumble sales, charity shops and car boot sales. Your craft space should be your very own personal space that you can use to further your brand.

Devise a versatile storage system that you can adapt according to your changing needs. Hooks, rods and other items can be repurposed, such as towel racks for ribbon spools. Work out what items are pleasing to look at and have them on show for inspiration.

Anchor the room with a spacious, centrally located work station. Choose a large, durable table with lots of space to work on (see page 30 for how to make your own). Glue a measuring tape to the edge for easy sizing.

*Above: Hang spare material on hooks, which can be personalised according to your style and brand. **Below:** Tidy away ribbon ends using wooden spools (page 20).*

- A sturdy chair is crucial, and the more stylish it is, the better.

- In addition to natural and overhead lighting, consider more focused task lighting, which can be useful when it comes to small-scale projects.

- Avoid carpet and rugs — flooring should ideally be suitable for sweeping.

- Consider mobile storage so you can transport your materials easily.

- Designate a space in your craft area for items typically used in every project like scissors, glue guns and tape, and keep that space tidy. Store these items in an easy-to-access area, such as in a drawer or on a grid system over your work table. Seldom-used supplies can be stored out of sight but should be clearly labelled so that you can always find what you need quickly.

- To get the most out of your crafting area, utilise all of the available space, whether it is over the door or even under a bed or table. You will be amazed at how much space you can create for storing your organised supplies.

- Hanging fabric and other large scraps can be the most effective way to store them, as it is much easier to rifle through them this way than as piles of fabric in boxes or baskets.

# MEET THE CRAFTERS
## EMMA LAMB

Emma Lamb is a textile artist, blogger and online shop owner who works from her home studio in Edinburgh, Scotland. She studied printed textiles at Edinburgh College of Art before embarking on a ten-year career in commercial textile designing. Her signature style was deeply rooted in traditional craft. Working directly with fabric, Emma would appliqué, embroider, crochet, knit, print and hand-embellish each concept design.

*'I am an absolute sucker for vintage tins, pretty floral bowls and patterned boxes; all of which are great for storing threads, buttons, yarns and the rest of my craft supplies – the perfect way to fuel my addiction for them!'*

In 2008 she became disillusioned with the speed at which the commercial markets 'churned' through design trends and went in search of a more sustainable and meaningful path of creativity. This is when she returned to the skills her mother had taught her as a child and began to focus heavily on both knitting and crochet.

1  *Neatly roll up your paper and store it in a waste paper bin or a washing basket for easy access.*

# STORAGE SOLUTIONS

## ① CONTAINERS

- Prevent craft supplies rolling around in drawers by using non-slip drawer liners.

- Store tools in pretty tins and jars, which will be more visually inspiring. Keep them in a handy reachable position.

- Old boxes of all kinds can be repurposed and decorated to fit in with your stylish new scheme.

- Crockery picked up at car boot sales and jumble sales can be used to display your favourite supplies.

- Use the containers you already have. Repurpose them and get inventive with upcycling and restoration.

## ② TIDYING

- Always put it back.

- Build in room to grow.

- Take an inventory.

- Put photographs on customised storage containers to indicate contents.

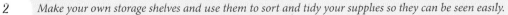

2  *Make your own storage shelves and use them to sort and tidy your supplies so they can be seen easily.*

3    *Use different shelves, drawers and colour-coded containers for each craft. Try to keep these different items confined to their assigned areas.*

4    *Make your craft space work for you by creating a truly inspirational area.*

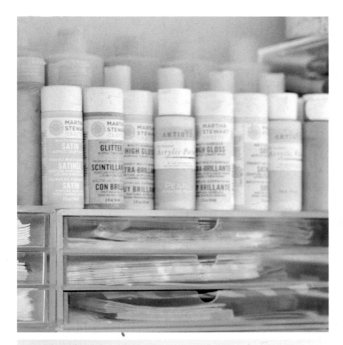

*Think of inventive storage solutions such as spice and wine racks.*

 **3** . . **ORGANISING**

- Create work stations for each activity.

- Go vertical with ceiling-high organised shelves and hooks.

- Label, label, label. Options include magnetic label holders and painted chalk labels.

- Categorise your things in a way that makes sense to you.

**4** . . **INSPIRATION**

- Keep inspiring art and past projects in sight to keep you motivated and creative.

- Look out for slide projector photo carousels that can be used to store inspiring images.

- Think about lighting.

**5** . . **BE PRACTICAL**

- Invest in or make a practical craft desk (page 30).

- Choose pretty but practical tools.

- Provide easy access to tools you use regularly.

- Use wall space cleverly – try storing your tools on a magnetic knife rack.

- Pegboards are one of the most versatile tools for organisation.

# HOW TO MAKE...

## RIBBON SPOOL HOLDER BOX

No more spools of ribbon unravelling and getting all tangled up! String the spools along a dowel with the ribbon ends feeding out through eyelet holes on one or both long sides of your box, depending on how many spools fit inside. Stack two or more of these boxes if needed and all your ribbons will be easy to find and dispense.

*1.* Find or make a suitable rectangular box, such as a photo storage box or a shoebox. Put the ribbon spools on the dowels to make sure that your ribbon supplies will all fit into the box before starting. The ribbons should all be on their original rounds; if not, make circular holders out of cardboard.

*2.* Mark where the dowel will need to hang from and affix a small cardboard cutout to the inside so the dowel can hang.

*3.* Cover your box in a paper of your choice (page 26).

*4.* Decide how many openings (eyelet holes) will be needed for the ribbons. Each ribbon that goes inside the box will need an opening.

*5.* Use small eyelets for narrow ribbons and large ones for wide ribbons. Mark where each size of eyelet will go on the box, along the longest sides of the box. The placement will correspond to where the ribbon round sits in the box, so make sure you have this already worked out.

*6.* Punch holes in the side of the box and set the eyelets, following the instructions with the eyelet kit. (Usually you would make a hole using a craft knife, small drill or scissors, and then attach each eyelet with the eyelet punch.)

*7.* Place dowels inside box and pull each ribbon through its respective eyelet so that it streams out of the box. Put the lid on the box and it's ready to use.

### TOOLS & MATERIALS
- Cardboard rectangular box
- Dowels (trim to box length)
- Cardboard
- Decorative paper
- Eyelets (small and large)
- Eyelet punch

1

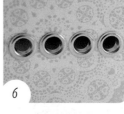
3

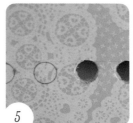
5

6

7

7

# WOODEN RIBBON SPOOL HOLDER

Surrounding yourself with neatly organised craft materials can help you stay creative and inspired. For a pretty and practical way to keep your ribbons in order, this quick and easy wooden spool holder is just the ticket. You can also match the colour to your brand design and decor for chic styling. Why not make a few and group your ribbons into inspiring colour palettes or themes?

*1.* Start by carefully drilling a hole the same width as your dowel in the centre of your coaster. Push the dowel into the drilled hole and glue in place. Let it dry.

*2.* Drill the same size hole into the bottom of your wooden handle about three-quarters of the way through.

*3.* Check that your dowel is firmly glued to the coaster. Check that your handle fits well on top of the dowel.

*4.* Remove the handle. Paint the coaster, dowel and handle with a couple of coats of paint and allow to dry.

*5.* Slide your spools of ribbon onto the dowel and place handle on top.

## TOOLS & MATERIALS

- Round wooden coaster
- 25cm (10in) dowel
- Drill
- Wood glue
- Round wooden drawer handle
- Craft paint
- Paintbrush

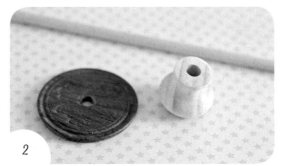

2

## TIPS

- To give it a shabby chic style, paint your spool holder white and add a top coat in a colour that you can lightly sand to give it a more worn look.

- To add glitz and glamour, use glitter craft paints or a metallic paint.

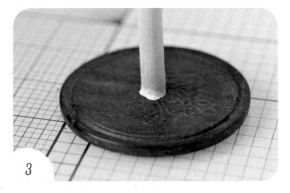

3

# MEET THE CRAFTERS
## HELENA SCHAEDER SÖDERBERG

Helena Schaeder Söderberg is the creator of the Craft & Creativity website and runs a shop called Make & Create. Creativity runs in her family. It started with her grandfather who was a watchmaker, an artist and inventor, and her mother is a craft fan and a skillful needle worker. A crafter all her life, Helena's best childhood memories are sitting by the kitchen table with her mum, making all kind of crafts. She still crafts with her mum, but now with the additional company of her two daughters.

Helena started posting pictures of her crafts and home on Flickr many years ago, and people kept asking her if she had a blog. In September 2011 she started Craft & Creativity and began filling it with craft and DIY tutorials. Craft & Creativity soon became a very popular blog and people kept asking her where to find the material she used in her crafts. That got her thinking that she should open a shop with her favourite craft supplies. Make & Create was born, and together with her colleague Jon, she runs a successful online shop. Helena lives with her two daughters, her husband and their cats in Vallentuna, Sweden.

*'I love that my space is so organised and that I can easily find what I want. On one wall I pin inspiration, in the form of postcards, prints and pieces of fabric. Since I'm a tidy crafter I like to have boxes or jars for everything. I even store ribbon scraps in old Tic Tac® containers.'*

## PRETTY PEN POTS

Turn tins into pretty storage pots by covering them with decorative paper – a quick, easy and cheap idea that will keep your pens, pencils and brushes neatly tidied away while making a great creative statement.

**TOOLS & MATERIALS**

- Empty tin
- Pretty paper or cardstock
- Double-sided tape
- Scissors
- Spray paint (optional)
- Washi tape (optional)

*1.* Wash and dry the empty tin. Cut a piece of printed card the size of your tin (you can use the old tin label as a template).

*2.* Cover the outside of the tin with strips of the double-sided tape.

*3.* Remove backing from tape and carefully wrap paper around tin. Fill with paint brushes, pencils or pens.

## TIPS

- Why not cover Pringles tins with pretty paper? They come with a lid too.

- Alternatively, spray with spray paint according to the paint instructions and allow to dry.

- Adhere washi tape to the tin in your desired pattern.

# HOW TO MAKE...

## COVERED BOX

Keeping your craft room clutter-free and inspiring requires stylish storage solutions. The fabric-covered storage box is a perfect fit as it can be personalised to your colour and style scheme and is also a great place for accessible storage.

*1.* Start by removing all the metal fittings from the base and lid of your wooden box.

*2.* Measure the bottom and sides of the box and add extra allowance to each side so the fabric will cover the inside of the box. Cut the fabric to this size.

*3.* Cover the top of the box lid with a thin but even layer of glue and wait a short while until the glue gets tacky.

*4.* Set box top on fabric to adhere. Cut uniform slits in the fabric at the corners so it will fold correctly. To do this, align a ruler flush against one side of the box. Draw a pencil line extending beyond the box edge (along the inside edge of the ruler). Cut along the line. Repeat for the other three corners.

*5.* Cover the sides of the box lid with a thin but even layer of glue and wait a short while until the glue gets tacky.

*6.* Bring one long side of fabric up and adhere to the box. Cover the sides of the inside box lid with glue as described in the previous step.

*7.* Fold the fabric into the box lid and restore metal fittings. Repeat on other long side. Repeat steps 2–7 with the short ends.

### TIP

- If the sides of the end flaps of fabric are fraying, dab some white glue along the cut edge of the fabric. It will dry clear and stop the fabric from fraying.

### TOOLS & MATERIALS

- Wooden box with metal fittings
- White glue
- Fabric
- Pencil
- Scissors
- Screwdriver

*1*

*3*

*5*

*6*

*7*

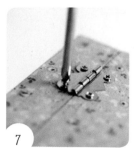

*7*

# HOW TO MAKE...

## STYLISH STORAGE BOXES

Create some stylish boxes for storing your scraps and leftover materials. This ensures they are easily found and remain clean and tidy without being visible.

*1.* Lay the paper on a working surface, pattern-side down. Place the box on the paper, leaving enough space on each side of the box for the paper to be able to fold up and cover each side.

*2.* Use the pencil to trace around the bottom of the box. Turn the box onto each side and also trace those edges.

*3.* Cut out around the outside of your trace marks, leaving about 6mm (¼in) of extra paper, just to make sure you have plenty of paper to cover the box.

*4.* Once you have cut out the large piece of paper, place the box back in the centre, using a little double-sided tape to hold it in place, and fold up each edge and crease.

*5.* Cut from each corner of the paper at an angle to each corner of the box. Then, using the creases as your guide, cut straight into each corner. Be sure that you cut straight in on opposite sides of the box (as shown) so that two sides of the box will end up with pointed flaps and two sides will end up with simple straight flaps.

*6.* Use mounting tape to add a strip of adhesive to the top edge of the outside of the box on the two sides with the pointed flaps of paper. Fold up these two sides firmly. Next, add mounting tape to the remaining two sides and fold up those flaps as well. Use scissors to trim the extra paper neatly around the edge of the box.

*7.* Repeat the steps on the box lid and you will have a beautifully covered box.

### TOOLS & MATERIALS

- Square or rectangular box
- Scrapbook paper/gift wrap/ wallpaper
- Pencil
- Scissors
- Double-sided tape
- Mounting tape or a similar strong double-sided adhesive tape

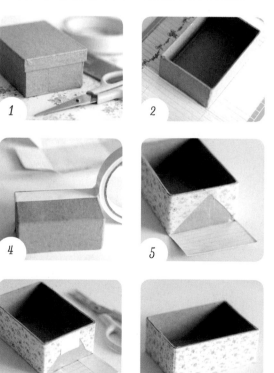

1

2

4

5

6

7

## CRAFT DESK

You need to anchor your workspace with a good table. There is a way to make one just like the high-end designer styles but much cheaper. Essentially, it is comprised of two counter-height backless bookcases or several small bookcases that support a table top. It can be adapted to be used in almost any space and it can be moved easily. Just work out what size you need and buy the bookcases and table top accordingly. To give it a personal stylish touch, adhere a laser-cut wood panel on the sides cut to your specific requirements. The best part about this table is that it has lots of storage space and as much work top as you have space for.

*1.* You need to start by finding bookcases that are tall enough, so around 100cm (40in) high. If you can't find any, you can always combine a couple of sets of shelves by joining them together using wood glue or dowel pegs. Then you will need to find a table with a table-top depth which is the same width as the shelves and long enough to tuck a stool or chair underneath.

*2.* If you want to add a decorative panel to the sides, find a laser-cut wood supplier and send them your design and measurements so you can work with them to get the finished result you want.

*3.* Start by assembling your bookcases or shelves according to the instructions.

*4.* Using a wood glue, lightly and evenly coat the back of the decorative wooden panels.

*Continued on page 32*

### TOOLS & MATERIALS
- White bookcases or self-supporting shelving (cube shelves work really well as they are nice and deep)
- Table top
- Dowel pegs x 2
- Wood glue
- Laser-cut wood panel x 2 (cut to the width and height of the shelf sides)

### TIP
- Paint the desk afterwards using several light coats for an even covering.

*1*     *2*     *4*

## CRAFT DESK (continued...)

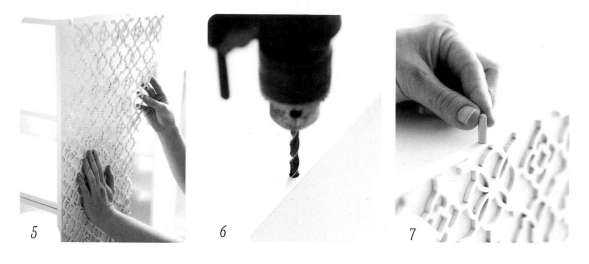

5      6      7

*5.* Carefully position and adhere wood panels to the side of your bookcase and leave to dry.

*6.* Drill a small hole in the top of each of your bookcases.

*7.* Insert a dowel peg.

*8.* Drill a coordinating hole in the underside of your table top.

*9.* Place table top on bookcases, securing it in place by lining up the dowel pegs to the holes in your table top.

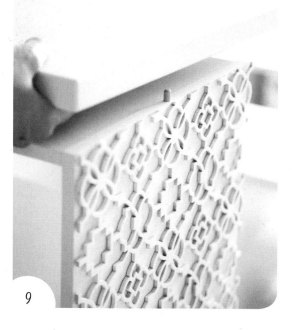

9

## UPCYCLED STORAGE JARS

These jars look great and are perfect to store your craft supplies in. They can be made in a variety of sizes to suit your storage needs.

### TOOLS & MATERIALS
- Plastic animal toys
- Glass jars with lids (cleaned and labels removed)
- Superglue
- Spray paint

*1.* Start by carefully gluing a plastic animal toy to a jar lid and set aside to dry.

*2.* Place the lid on a platform you no longer need (I used an old glass pot I did not need anymore). Following the instructions on the spray paint, carefully spray the glued animal and lid until you have an even coat of paint and the original colour of both the animal and lid are no longer visible. Allow to dry.

*3.* Screw the painted lid onto the jar and use it to store all your small craft supplies.

*'It's helpful to have lots of colourful bowls, jars, tins, or anything that could be used for storing small craft pieces. They will keep you organised and will also look nice as display on your shelves.'*
City Chic Country Mouse

1

2

# CREATIVE BOARDS

So now you've created an inspiring craft space to work in, and got your supplies organised and stored away – what's next? You need to put together a creative board.

There are two types of creative boards: mood boards and inspiration boards. They are both a collage of images, textures, words and objects that a designer has collected and wants to organise and keep as a reference for ongoing projects. They come in many forms, from a paper poster, a notice board or a digital graphic, to any other visual medium. They are used in all branches of design, from fashion, architecture, fine arts, event planning, websites, graphic and game design, and they help develop design concepts and communicate ideas to other members of a design team or to clients.

But how do they differ? A mood board sets the mood. It's a way of harnessing and illustrating inspiration and ideas that convey a feeling, style, ambience or context of how a product will make you feel. Start to think in a conceptual way – it's all about feeling and psychology.

An inspiration board is more specific and visual. It is a collection of references or prototypes for elements that will eventually feature in the designed project. Inspiration boards are more literal. Think about details, colours, forms, textures and lines.

In summary, a mood board gathers all the research and images of how the product will make you feel, and an inspiration board gathers all the reference points for what the product will look like. The mood board should influence what goes on to the inspiration board and the inspiration board should respond to the mood board.

They are both intuitive ways to brainstorm and organise the ideas you really like, and help you stay focused, filter your thoughts and keep your ideas and designs together. They can give a voice to the ideas trapped in your head. You can make small changes or completely change direction without already having invested a lot of time and effort in starting the actual design work. If you are working with other people, creative boards bring clarity to the project. What one person considers romantic, another may not. By adding visual images and swatches, etc., to go with your words, the board becomes much more specific. If you are working in a team, everyone can coordinate their ideas more easily. The boards are especially helpful if you are hiring someone to help you with the graphics and web design of your brand.

---

**Below:** *This alternative mood board makes good use of wire and clips to display inspirational material without damaging it with pins and tape.*

# WHY MAKE A CREATIVE BOARD?

- It's a fun way to get the creative juices flowing.

- It's a way of organising those shimmers of colours or vague ideas; a way of dreaming up solutions for specific challenges, like how you will set yourself apart from other crafters.

- Often we think we know what we like or want to portray but have a hard time focusing or narrowing down our concepts. This is where the mood and inspiration boards can help. Ask any professional designer if creative boards serve a useful purpose and the answer is always yes.

- They are a great way to identify the colours you gravitate toward; a method of envisioning your design project in its early stages to enable you to clarify your needs.

You can find ideas in magazines and online, pick up paint swatches from your local DIY shop, and gather up buttons, embroidery threads and other helpful items. Free postcards, interesting bits of paper, wallpaper swatches, coloured masking tape, stamps, stickers, fabric swatches and so on can all go in. Boards are fun, easy, and can be done with your hands or on a computer, often without costing a penny!

Why not make a mood board before you start decorating your craft area? That way your brand will begin to synchronise with all the creative inspiration around you.

First of all, you will want to plan your mood board. What kind of a mood are you going for; what is it going to be about; and what is the purpose, end goal or dream your board needs to inspire? On the subject of branding, what do you want your brand to say about you? What's the emotion that you want your product launch or website to generate: playful and lighthearted, warm and endearing, glamorous and sophisticated? How are you going to communicate the mood?

Start by gathering up all your initial images, ideas and finds and spreading them out on the floor, a board or a large table. Start moving them around and seeing how everything works together. Then start tearing interesting images from magazines or printing interesting images you find on the Internet to plug gaps or hammer out ideas and pull the concept together. Look for imagery that 'speaks' to your design aesthetic. When you have all your images and finds laid out, you often find that a pattern will reveal itself. You'll see certain materials and colours you are attracted to, ones you prefer over the others. Approach the task with a light and playful heart and a mood will come to you. Keep taking a step back from your ideas and simply observe. Discard anything that doesn't flow. Keep moving things around, playing with contrast and textures – happy accidents occur when you just go with the flow.

The next step is to find a platform for your board, ideally one that can be mounted on a vertical surface for easy viewing. Supports can come in all shapes and sizes, so decide whether you want to make a pin board or clipboard that you can change, or a collaged poster or digital board. You can use a cork board or a large sheet of craft board. Other alternatives include hanging a curtain wire and using the clips to suspend your inspiration in the air. Use washi tape to adhere your finds to a blank wall, or you can use your computer to make a digital version. You could also make a magnetic board or ribbon board.

If you ever want to share your board online, you'll want to choose public domain images to avoid breaching copyright. If you have a copyrighted image that you love, try hunting on Flickr for Creative Commons work (page 123).

Take a photo of your board so you can carry it around with you. Keep looking at it so you can be sure you're on the right track.

Use an inspiration board to inspire the graphics for your branding. Images might include other works of art you admire, your favourite print, or textures and patterns you are often drawn to. Text might include quotes or just words that are specific to your brand. Generally your boards aren't trying to be a work of art but rather a collection of images and ideas that inspire. Having said that, I am sure you will still want it to look great and be a pleasing composition, so sort and trim the pieces for your board. Larger images work well as a base and a variety of sizes can look very effective. Remember you don't need an abundance of materials, just a select few that tell your story.

So now you have an organised craft area, a mood board that sums up your brand, and an inspiration board to project the mood and feeling of your brand, why not start branding your craft area? And no, I don't mean putting up signs and banners. You can brand your craft space in a much more subtle way, as shown in the crafter profiles in this book. Take Vicky Trainor, for example (page 97), her brand is about bright and bold primary colours, and Wit & Whistle's clean lined stationery is reflected in clean lines and a super-organised space.

If you know my brand, Torie Jayne, you will be familiar with my pretty pastels, modern look and touches of vintage. So in my craft room, I have acrylic drawers alongside a vintage filing cabinet, modern shelves with stainless steel ends, and quirky glass jars.

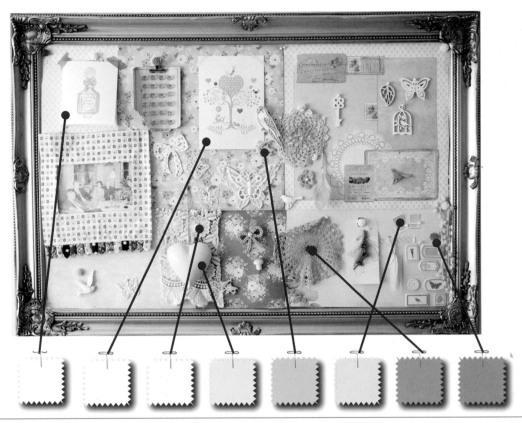

*Above:* When you have all your ideas and images laid out, you will be able to narrow down your colour palette and see how different shades, hues and tones work together to inspire your next project as well as your branding.

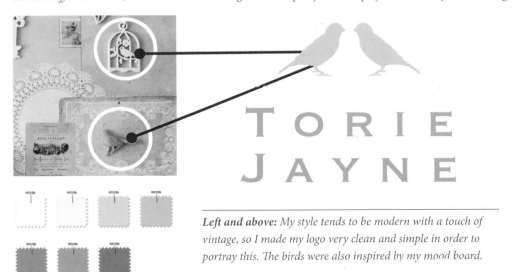

*Left and above:* My style tends to be modern with a touch of vintage, so I made my logo very clean and simple in order to portray this. The birds were also inspired by my mood board.

# TIPS

- Magazine tear sheets have a tendency to buckle, so print a copy for best results. This also enables you to re-size them.

- Spray adhesives work well on cardstock, but remember to use them in a well-ventilated area and use old newspaper as a background as they can get very messy.

- If you don't like to use pins, magnets are a good option. You can find magnetic surfaces at charity shops and DIY shops.

- Paint charts from your local hardware shop are great for colour inspiration.

- Don't restrict yourself to just imagery; add anything that evokes mood or texture.

- The only rule with creating boards is there are no rules, so give your creativity free rein.

# INSPIRATIONAL MATERIALS

- Texts
- Poems
- Magazine tear sheets
- Ribbons
- Threads
- Beads
- Buttons
- Small toys
- Junk jewellery
- Dried flowers
- Maps
- Train, plane and concert tickets
- Shells
- Anything and everything that captures a mood

## MEET THE CRAFTERS
## ELYSE MAJOR

Elyse Major is the creator of the brand Tinkered Treasures. Elyse has always loved making pretty handcrafted objects, and has indulged her love of all things artistic while working as a communications consultant and also as a mother and homemaker.

*'I am inspired by others doing what they love, whether it's marvelling at an author orchestrating a large craft fair or watching my boys invent their own comic book characters. My ideas can be seen in a variety of places, including the sticky notes on my wall and even in my phone notepad.'*

She began blogging about her adventures in DIY several years ago and rediscovered her love of creating. An accomplished writer, in addition to her book, *Tinkered Treasures*, Elyse regularly contributes features and articles to magazines such as *Romantic Homes*, *Romantic Country*, and *French Country Style*. Elyse is a married mum of two creative boys and lives in Rhode Island, USA.

## DECORATIVE DRAWING PINS

Dress up your inspiration boards with these cute drawing pins to hang your notes, papers and ideas. In very little time you can have a notice board covered with colourful birds, flowers or other brand ideas that add a touch of colour and quirkiness to your boards.

### TOOLS & MATERIALS

- Drawing pins
- Resin cabochon shapes that represent your brand
- Superglue

When selecting your cabochons consider your colours and brand design, as these small items are an extremely effective way of extending your brand within your craft space.

Ensure your drawing pins are smaller than the items you wish to decorate them with. Simply glue the flat top of the drawing pin to the cabochon and let it dry.

### TIP

- You could make your own cabochons using a silicone mould and modelling clay, available from most craft supply outlets (page 130).

toriejayne.blogspot.com/

toriejayne@gmail.com

www.etsy.com/#!/TorieJayne

twitter.com/TorieJayne

pinterest.com/toriejayne

www.flickr.com/photos/toriejayne

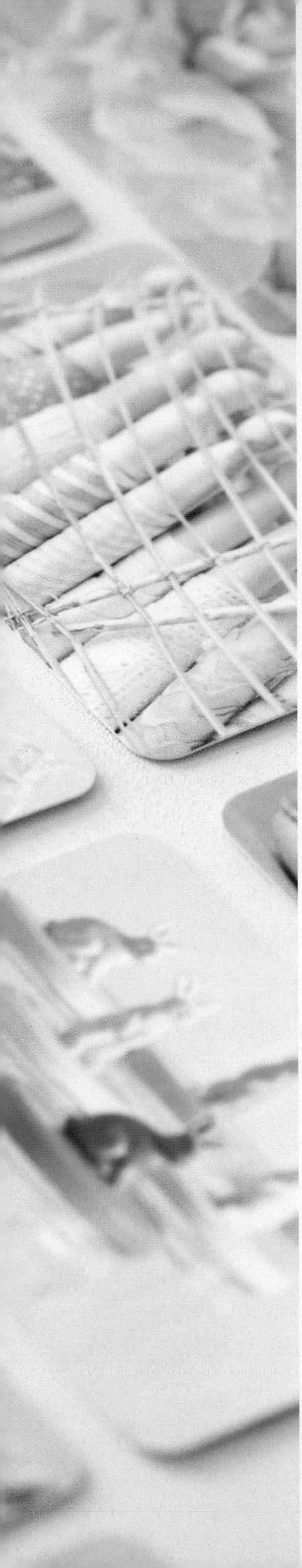

# CHAPTER 2
# BRANDING

Personality matters. A strong brand name and design, a powerful online profile across various social media platforms, professional images, and stylish stationery and packaging can all make a huge difference to your brand. I'll show you how to build your brand so that it is instantly recognisable, which can attract new customers and draw loyal customers back for more.

# CONDUCTING MARKET RESEARCH

**M**arket research is a vital part of building any business, and it is the first thing you should do when starting out. It can give you a picture of what kinds of new products may bring a profit as well as continued success for existing businesses. It might seem like a mystery, a big-business luxury, or something that is complex and hard to do. It's not. It basically boils down to the process of looking at what people want to buy and in what quantities, to see if you will be able to meet your requirements. It is smart research and evaluation of the data you collect. By researching the answers to specific questions, you can also learn whether you need to change your package design or tweak your delivery methods, and even find the best place to sell your crafts.

When you conduct market research, you can use the results either to create a craft business and marketing plan or to measure the success of your current plan. Flaws you find in your grand plan will be much easier to correct at the start of the process than further down the line. That is why it is important to ask the right questions, in the right way, of the right people. Every business needs to know what products are needed or wanted, the target audience to reach, the best way to offer goods to potential customers, and how to hold on to current customers. Poor research can steer a business in the wrong direction, so don't panic if the results are not exactly what you wanted or expected – adapting is part of the process. Remember, opinions are rarely static and therefore are likely to change over time, so it is well worth repeating your research at different stages in your business start-up and beyond.

There are two main types of research, primary and secondary.

- Primary research is the information that you personally collect from people and then analyse. This can be done through interviews, questionnaires or surveys, by telephone, email, social media channels or face to face.

- Secondary research is information already gathered by someone else and published as a report or an article.

Before you jump in and spend a lot of your hard-earned money and valuable time on market research, here are some basic mistakes to avoid and questions to ask to help you get started.

## COMMON MARKETING MISTAKES

- Using only secondary research.

- Using only web resources.

- Surveying only the people you know.

- Only listening to positive feedback about your craft business or brand idea. (You also need to listen to those who are critical.)

## SURVEYS

When conducted well, surveys can reap great rewards, but how do you go about conducting a successful survey? My first suggestion would be to use an online survey tool like SurveyMonkey (www.surveymonkey.com), which has the added bonus of reporting options and can sort the data for you.

When composing the questions you will ask in your survey, ask yourself if you really need the answer to each question. You want to keep your surveys short and sweet, with simple and specific questions. Be sure to add statistical questions such as age, location, etc., and to include a progress bar to keep your respondents engaged. Inform them from the beginning how long it will take them to take the survey. Try to phrase questions so they are open-ended, allowing your respondents to answer in their own words, without preconceived notions.

After you have conducted your initial research and collected all your findings and data, carefully analyse by looking at the results. Compile a summary of what you have learned. With this information, you will be able to adjust your craft business ideas to make it more of a success.

## QUESTIONS TO ASK

- What do you think about this craft?

- Would you be willing to buy this?

- What would you be willing to pay for this?

- Where do you expect to buy this?

- Have you bought something similar in the past?

- If so, where did you buy it?

## THINGS TO CONSIDER

- Are your craft products just like hundreds of others out there? If so, how can you make your craft products stand out? Research what your competition is offering, and then plan how to make your crafts stand out from the crowd.

- Visit your national statistics or census website to find out information on everything from people's spending habits to how prices change; this is all free market data.

# MAKING A BUSINESS PLAN

You need a plan to succeed. Think of it as a road map to success. You need to know where you're going and how you're going to get there to be successful. When you start to write your business plan, it will really help with your market research in order to find out what you want to know.

Starting a craft business is more than spending your day pursuing your hobby. By taking a professional approach to making and selling your crafts, you can make your dream a reality. You obviously have a passion for crafts, but you should not overlook the importance and merits of having a solid plan that backs up your interests.

A great place to start is with a good business plan that lays out what you want to do and how you want to do it, because the better you plan the more successful

you will be. Let's face it, there are very few people who simply stumble on financial success.

A good business plan is great at focusing the mind, clarifying your business idea and defining your long-term objectives. It will provide a blueprint for running your business and a series of benchmarks for checking your progress.

In its most basic form, a business plan is a written description of the future of your business, a document that tells you what you plan to do and how you plan to do it. This living document generally projects three to five years ahead and outlines the route you intend to take to grow your revenue. It's a useful document to constantly refer back to as your business grows, and when done well will serve as a continual guide to help you realise your dreams.

# MEET THE CRAFTERS
## ANNABELLE OZANNE

Annabelle Ozanne is the creator of textile artwork brand Three Red Apples. Annabelle's love of creating started in her dad's huge workshop in Brittany, France, where she was born. At a turning point in her life, Annabelle was looking for a career change and discovered freehand machine embroidery.

*'Crafting keeps traditional skills alive,*
*an important thing in my book.*
*There is definitely room in our world for*
*new technologies and old ones to live side*
*by side and mingle occasionally.'*

In her previous creative job as a web designer Annabelle had been using the computer as her creative tool, but she felt a yearning to start using her hands to create. She loved the idea of drawing with a needle, so she started with an embroidery foot and got stitching, quickly finding the doodling motion itself very addictive, and then started adding to the design with paint to accentuate patterns and colours on vintage fabrics. Annabelle lives in Devon, England.

# BRAND BUILDING

Branding can seem like a scary word associated with corporate culture, but it doesn't have to be. In simplest terms, a brand is a promise to customers. It is the overall impression your customers have about your business and the products you offer. With every interaction it sets expectations for what they'll get from you and your products.

Conveying your brand amounts simply to living it and delivering it to the world. As a crafter, while you may have logos and brand names, at the end of the day you are the living, breathing embodiment of your brand. Everywhere you go and everything you do represents your brand and invites the public to assess it and engage with it. You can convey your brand personally, professionally, socially and in every other

imaginable way, and you will do it online and offline. You will become the brand you have envisioned. You will live it, breathe it and deliver it everywhere you go, as it is naturally an extension of you.

Your brand is going to become the foundation of your business, allowing you to distinguish yourself from all the other crafters. Of all the well-known crafters, all their brands have one thing in common – they are an extension of the crafters' personalities. In this chapter we will look at successful crafters' brands and see how their personalities shine through them.

Remember your point of differentiation is the uniqueness of yourself and your product, so play this up in any way you can and don't be afraid to let your true colours literally shine through.

# DEFINING YOUR BRAND

Design the elements of your brand identity so you have visual representations to use on your packaging, online profiles and business stationery, to name just a few. These elements include your logo, colour palette, theme and typefaces. Use them everywhere you can, so people consistently see your brand visually, which in time will boost brand awareness, recognition, loyalty and advocacy. The more cohesive and appealing your branding, the more likely buyers are to browse your shop, read your blog, and follow and 'like' you on social networking sites.

First, create an inspiration board of all your ideas, words, images, names, colours, prints, packaging – just about anything you feel relates to your craft business. You can do this on a blank wall using washi tape, on a

pinboard or in a big scrapbook. Don't try to copy the look or style of someone else's brand. However, looking at other brands may help spark some ideas for your own.

The plan is to add and remove gradually until you have created an inspirational representation of your brand vision that both excites and informs everything your craft business does, big or small. Consider what you want to communicate about your brand. Your graphics are going to write a story without words. Try jotting down words that describe your shop style.

Branding can appear in various sizes depending on your products and platforms, but remember it must work as a whole in order for your work to be instantly recognisable.

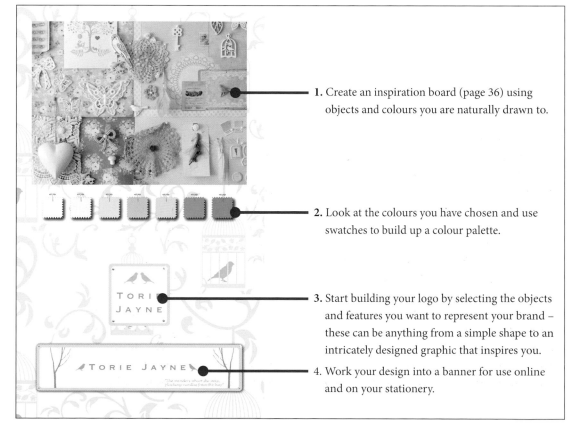

1. Create an inspiration board (page 36) using objects and colours you are naturally drawn to.

2. Look at the colours you have chosen and use swatches to build up a colour palette.

3. Start building your logo by selecting the objects and features you want to represent your brand – these can be anything from a simple shape to an intricately designed graphic that inspires you.

4. Work your design into a banner for use online and on your stationery.

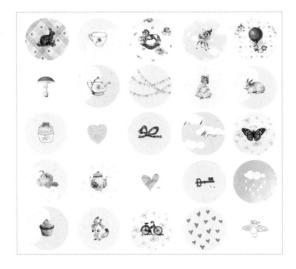

*Above:* A selection of signature buttons from Tabitha Emma (page 113).

*Above:* Amanda Wright's hive postcard (page 58).

## CRAFTERS' STYLES

- 'A Feminine Rock romantic on the childish whimsical side.' Anne Cresci, Matilou (page 107)

- 'Cute, sassy, melancholy, pastel, punchy.' Mel Stringer, Girlie Pains (page 75)

- 'Clean, simple and organic.' Amanda Wright, Wit & Whistle (page 58)

- 'Eclectic, whimsical style, with a pinch of humour at times.' Annabelle Ozanne, Three Red Apples (page 49)

- 'I would describe my style as a floral gathering of makings with a nod to the arts and crafts, the make-do-and-mend ethos of the forties and a personal love of flower arranging in fabric.' Vicky Trainor (page 97)

*Above:* The embroidery doodles of Annabelle Ozanne (page 49).

# MEET THE CRAFTERS
## STUDIO SNOWPUPPE

Nellianna van den Baard, Kenneth Veenenbos and Fleur van Dusseldorp are the creative force behind origami lamp company Studio Snowpuppe. Nellianna is an architect who loves making beautiful products that contribute to the world's wellbeing, and whose father taught her the beauty of pleating paper. Kenneth is an industrial designer who is inspired by nature, and Fleur is an urban planner turned paper engineer who loves to bake.

*'Every design is like a puzzle.*
*When we start we can't stop until*
*the puzzle has been finished.'*

Snowpuppe creates lampshades from parchment paper that diffuse a smooth and cosy light. These geometric paper lampshades are made from flat pieces of paper which are turned into intricate-looking sculptural pieces using precise and detailed folds.

Together with their cats June and Ayla, Snowpuppe work from their studio in The Hague, designing, manufacturing and shipping their beautiful lampshades containing minimal resources and natural materials all over the world.

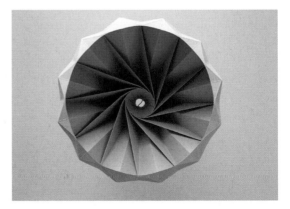

# BRAND
# COLOURS

One of the key elements of building a strong brand is colour selection. Integrating your brand colours in your logo, landing pages, product and more will help you achieve the highest impact from your brand.

Every colour has a different feeling and various associations. Colours will evoke certain emotions and feelings towards your brand, so it is vital to choose colours that will represent your identity effectively. You want your colour palette to speak to your potential customers about who you are and the way you work.

Start by thinking about what colours you are naturally drawn to on your inspiration board, what colours appear most frequently, and which colours work with your craft products. Which colours do you find delightful, love and can live happily with? Then gather those shades and tones of colours in a selection of paint swatches from your local hardware shop or create a virtual palette using a design software package.

Next, narrow down your colour palette by choosing four to six colours for your brand: one to two main colours, and three to four accent colours.

Tape or pin your refined colours to a board and keep looking at it as you ask yourself: do the colours best represent the feel of your products or the image you hope to project? Do they reflect the emotional response you wish to portray with your brand? Are they suitable to the gender and age of your potential customers?

Keep working with your colour palette until you fall in love with what it says about you and your brand. Then, use your new branding colours – and only these colours – throughout your blog design, logo and packaging to create a professional-grade branding palette.

## COLOUR TERMINOLOGY

**Shades** are created by adding varying amounts of black to a colour to make it darker.

**Tones** are created when grey is added to colours, resulting in colours that are less intense.

**Tints** are created by adding white to a pure colour to make it lighter.

**An accent colour** is a colour used in quite small quantities to lift or to add punch to a colour scheme.

## PRIMARY COLOURS

Primary colours are three key colours – red, blue and yellow. They cannot be made from any other colour.

## COMPLEMENTARY COLOURS

Pick a colour on the colour wheel and draw a straight line across the colour wheel. This is the colour's complement. These colours are basically opposites and serve to contrast and reinforce each other. Look at the colour wheel and you will see the left-hand side of the colours are 'warm' or 'hot' and the ones on the right are 'cool' or 'cold'.

## SECONDARY COLOURS

If you mix equal amounts of the primary colours, you get the secondary colours – purple, green and orange.

## TERTIARY COLOURS

If you mix a primary with a secondary colour in a ratio of 2:1, you get a tertiary colour – red with orange, blue with green, etc.

## ANALOGOUS COLOURS

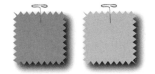

This is when you select a colour on the colour wheel that is next to the colour you are choosing. One colour is used as a dominant colour while others are used to enrich the scheme.

## TRIAD COLOURS

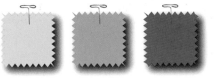

Choose a colour on the colour wheel then draw an equilateral triangle to find the two other colours. This scheme offers strong visual contrast while retaining balance and richness of colour.

## FEELING AND ASSOCIATIONS

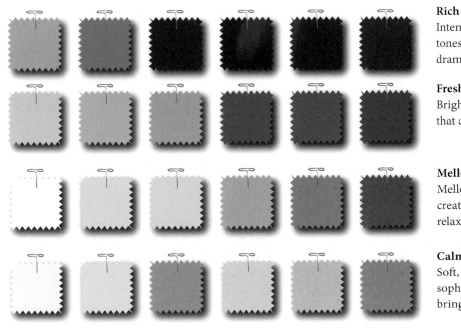

**Rich**
Intense, dark-to-mid tones that create a dramatic feel

**Fresh**
Bright to pastel shades that are uplifting

**Mellow**
Mellow colours that create a cosy and relaxed ambience

**Calm**
Soft, muted and sophisticated colours that bring a sense of calm

# MEET THE CRAFTERS
## AMANDA WRIGHT

Amanda Wright is the creator of paper goods brand Wit & Whistle. After graduating, Amanda spent three years working as a company designer, but it wasn't scratching her creative itch. She started to become despondent at all the tweaks and changes she would have to make for clients, which resulted in her not recognising the final designs. So she started designing her own paper products on the side. Wit & Whistle offers witty greeting cards and whistle-worthy paper goods – all designed and illustrated by Amanda.

*'I chose my brand name because I started out making witty, whistle-worthy greeting cards.'*

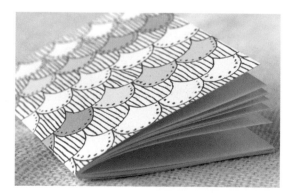

When she's not inventing new goodies to sell, Amanda tries to make sure life is brimming with creative moments, by doodling in her sketchbook, dreaming up DIY projects, getting dirt under her fingernails in the garden, dabbling in photography, and cooking and baking. Amanda lives with her husband, Daniel, in a quirky A-frame house in Cary, North Carolina with their two dogs, Oliver and Mabel.

# IT'S ALL IN A NAME

The unique name you choose for your brand should reflect the image you want to project to your market. Pick one that is easy to remember and pronounce. Do your research to make sure that it is not already in use and is available as a web address and across social media platforms you intend to use. Take the time to research how it will work on your branding, packaging and business stationery. Write it without spaces to see how it would look as an email address and on social networking sites. You want your brand name to engage your customers emotionally and arouse their curiosity and interest. Your name should differentiate you from competitors and be memorable to your customers.

## NAME TYPES

- Descriptive name — a name that clearly describes the products you sell. For example, Whitney Smith Pottery is pottery made by Whitney Smith.

- Suggestive name — a name that alludes to the type of products you sell. For example, The Vintage Drawer, which is Vicky Trainor's craft brand, uses vintage fabrics and materials.

- Fanciful name — a name that can either be completely made-up with no inherent meaning, or real words used out of context. For example, Matilou is a combination of Anne Cresci's kids' names, Matis and Lou.

- Your name — this can be your full name, your first and middle name, first and last name, or all three. For example, Tabitha Emma Bray uses Tabitha Emma as her brand name.

*'I decided to use my first and middle name as it gave me the freedom to change my business, because the brand name always works, no matter what I choose to do. It also makes it easy to promote myself as a creator.'*
Tabitha Emma Bray,
Tabitha Emma

*'All my old fabrics, linens and haberdashery were stored in an old tall cupboard. At the top of this was a drawer that I labelled "the vintage drawer", so it was just a simple natural progression that my brand be named the same. The Linen Garden is the name of my blog and the title of my online haberdashery shop. This title is simply the name that I affectionately call my studio.'*
Vicky Trainor,
The Vintage Drawer

*'I have always liked the word "tinker" to describe the style of crafting I do because much of it is embellishing rather than constructing, and "treasures" followed as a natural fit after "tinkered" since I am a fan of alliteration.'*
Elyse Major,
Tinkered Treasures

# DESIGNING AN AVATAR

Your avatar is the little square picture or graphic you use to represent you or your brand on social media platforms.

On Facebook, Twitter, Instagram and Etsy, it is called a profile picture; on Pinterest it's a picture; and on Flickr it's called a buddy icon. Whatever it's called, it's essentially the same thing. It is your identification for online social media and quite often the first image a potential customer sees because it appears next to your tweets, Facebook posts and blog comments. Therefore, it is an important aspect of your social media presence.

It should become so familiar to your fans, followers and customers that they will quickly recognise it as they scan through the numerous updates of people they follow on social media. Use the same avatar on all of your social networking sites for a consistent professional brand awareness.

Resist the urge to continually change your profile picture. You want it to be etched into your followers' minds. Can you imagine McDonald's removing the arches from their brand or even changing their colours? Choose a photo, picture or graphic you love, as you do not want to grow tired of it.

There is a great website that lets you automate your profile picture when you are commenting on blogs. It's called gravatar.com. You will need to sign up to wordpress.com first, then you upload your profile picture and provide your email addresses. Then, whenever you are commenting on a blog by providing your email in the comment box, your profile picture at Gravatar will automatically be displayed. Another great way to keep your brand consistent!

What should you use for your avatar? Opinion differs widely on whether you should use a photo of yourself or your product or a brand logo. Some say the only problem with using a photo is that some images are a lot smaller than others and that it is a lot easier to identify a logo quickly. Also, a logo won't become dated like a photo does. Others will tell you that people don't 'connect' with a logo, they connect with a face. However, the most important thing is that your avatar is well planned and executed, and supports your overall brand by way of the graphics/photograph used, the use of text/company logo, or both. So I will leave it up to you to decide whether you use a great photo of yourself or your product or a well-designed logo.

*'Branding shouldn't be an afterthought. Make sure your avatar is a continuation of your brand – your customers will notice!'*
Amanda Wright

If you use a photo, you want it to be a high-quality image. A professional photographer – especially if you're having your photo taken – would be my recommendation. A professional photographer can help capture your personality and uniqueness. If your budget does not stretch to hiring a professional, ask someone you know who has an eye for good photography. Make sure your photo is crisp and clear. Look professional but not staid and unapproachable. Smile and make eye contact to communicate your desire to network and do business with your viewer.

If you're using a great photo of your best product, ensure the background is clean and neutral so that your product really stands out.

If you are using your own logo or graphic for your profile image, make sure it is simple, crisp and clear, yet memorable when scaled down.

Whether you use a photo or logo, your little square image needs to reflect your brand, so utilise your brand colours and style. You want to have an eye-catching picture that stands out so people know who you and your brand are on first sight.

## TIPS

- The profile picture is generally pretty small when it appears next to your comments, tweets, etc., but more often than not, can be viewed at its original size. Keep photos of yourself or your products at full size and design graphics larger than you need them because graphics scaled down retain quality while scaled-up images degrade.

- Square images are used by most social networks. The size may vary but the square proportion doesn't, so be certain to start with a square image. You will find that most of the network platforms allow you to upload a picture of just about any size and crop it, or they let you select the image area you would like to focus on as your square profile image. But if you are familiar with photo programs like Adobe® Photoshop® or free online resources such as PicMonkey, I would suggest you crop your image to a square first.

*Below: Three examples of eye-catching avatar images: a profile photograph, a brand logo and a product shot.*

# CHAPTER 3
# SELLING BASICS

Once you've built your brand – and made your chosen crafts, of course – it's time to get it out into the marketplace. This could include online, at a craft fair, in a shop, at a market or through a pop-up event or exhibition.

# WHERE TO SELL?

Traditionally, crafts were sold at lots of different venues like local art fairs, regional craft fairs, and galleries. But today millions of people are selling online. For some crafters, the Internet represents the major source of their income, while for others it is a way to generate some extra spending money. In any case, it is definitely worth considering online selling as part of your sales mix. However, deciding where to sell online can be a minefield, so I'll describe three of the main options for craft sellers.

Selling online with an established craft-focused e-commerce website that is dedicated to buying and selling crafts is one of the best and cheapest ways to generate sales all-year-round. Essentially, sellers post listings for the crafts they have for sale and customers browse and buy the items they like. The site facilitates the process by gathering multiple sellers in one place

and often providing payment-processing options.

But which site do you choose? Some crafters sell on more than one site to increase their exposure. Just be careful what you sell on the multiple sites, as you don't want to be seen selling the same unique item twice. I would advise starting with just one site, as managing listings on multiple sites will ultimately take more time and money.

With so many sellers on these sites, it is very important for you to stand out from all the other crafters doing the same thing. Organise your crafts into different categories. This will make it easy when you put your marketing into action and will also help you when it comes to setting up a stall and/or online shop.

The more types of items you have to sell online, the better. When customers have a variety of items to choose from, they will invariably spend more time browsing and they're more likely to purchase. Creating your own website can take a lot of time and money, so this is generally advisable for large sellers only.

When you are deciding which site to sell your craft on, you need to ask yourself several questions (see right). Most, if not all of these questions can be answered by online research, but also make sure you talk to other designers and makers, ask questions on forums, read comments on blog posts, etc.

Let's take a look at a few of the online options for selling your crafts:

- ETSY is the largest and most popular online market for selling crafts. It opened in 2005, is based in the US, and is a worldwide selling platform. The challenge with a huge site like Etsy is to find ways to stand out from the crowd and constantly relisting your goods in order to do so; on the positive side, however, there is already lots of traffic, with thousands of potential customers passing through. Setting up an Etsy shop is easy; you just need to personalise your space. They will handle search engine marketing, which enables customers to find your shopfront, but you will still need to do some marketing of your own.

*'In my view, Etsy is the best international handmade marketplace and is unrivalled in its ability to attract enthusiastic buyers and sellers; it encourages a supportive and energetic community spirit.'*
Emma Lamb

Etsy has great forums and advice pages where you can read about packaging, marketing and success stories. Facebook has an app that enables users to showcase their Etsy store in their profile or on their fan page.

## THINGS TO CONSIDER

- Research the charges. Is there a one-time joining fee or an annual subscription? Is there a listing fee? How much commission do they take?

- What payment options do they accept?

- How popular is the site with your target audience?

- What marketing do they do?

- How does the website look? Is it user-friendly?

- What are the price points for similar products to yours?

- How many international customers use the site? Will you be able to ship your goods to those customers cost-effectively?

- Who else is promoting the site?

- Do they have a community you can network with?

- How easy is it to leave?

- DAWANDA is another online marketplace for gifts and handmade products, which is based in Germany. It was started in 2006, has a more European focus, but like Etsy can be used by anyone.

- FOLKSY was created with the aim of showcasing the work of UK designers and makers. James Boardwell and Rob Lee came together to build Folksy in 2007 after being inspired by the energy in the craft communities in the UK as well as in North America and Australia. Folksy is now the largest marketplace for handmade work and focuses mainly on the UK.

# DESIGNING A VIRTUAL SHOP BANNER

When selling online, your banner is like the book title or shop sign and should prominently include your shop name. Your banner should clearly imply the kinds of items you sell. Consider including a tag line or additional words to describe your products.

Use imagery to communicate visually what your shop sells. Make sure your banner is designed to fill the specified dimensions, which are usually given in pixel size. Use your brand colours and make sure they really stand out on the page (page 54).

It's a good idea to incorporate your brand logo somewhere central so it immediately stands out to the customer. In the competitive online marketplace it needs to grab the customer's attention in a matter of seconds.

For demonstration purposes in this book only, we have created a fictitious handmade jewellery brand, *Maria Makes*, to help illustrate the principles behind online selling.

*'Stay true to your own ideals and skills and don't be too inspired by the industry you work in. It helps to ensure, in a certain way, that you stand out. Being creative means you are constantly spinning in your own whirlpool of ideas.'*
Vicky Trainor,
The Vintage Drawer

## TIPS

- Don't overcrowd the banner and choose items that best represent your brand and style. Prioritise quality over quantity.

- There are plenty of online tutorials to help you create a banner. Adobe® Photoshop® is a worthwhile investment.

- Alternatively, employ a designer to do the work for you.

- Enlarge and print the banner for your craft fair (page 92) or shop (page 106).

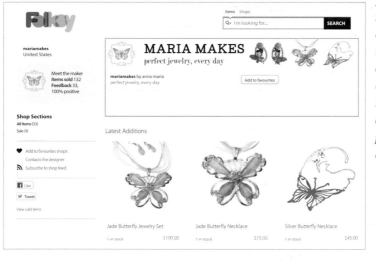

*Left and below: Your virtual shop could be a specialised website, but these can be expensive and time-consuming, especially for a small business. Instead, craft sites like Folksy and DaWanda offer you an established selling platform with easy pre-made templates to customise for own your personal brand.*

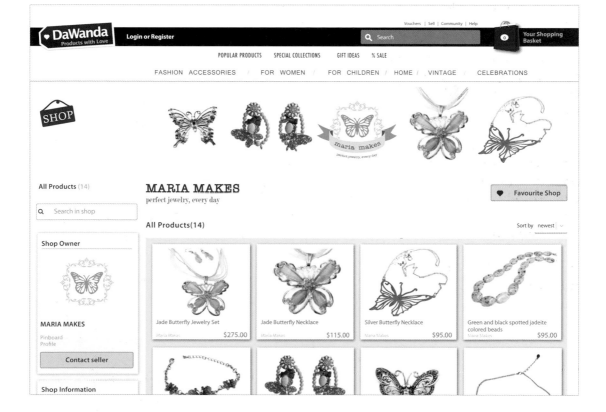

# MEET THE CRAFTERS
## TAMAR SCHECHNER

Tamar Schechner is the creator of handmade jewellery brand Nest Pretty Things. The daughter and grandchild of artists, she studied design at Parsons School of Design in New York. Eight years ago Tamar moved from Tel Aviv, Israel, to the state of Vermont, USA. In Israel she was creative director and fashion stylist at a magazine for more than eighteen years.

*'Selling online really works for me. It's very important to be visible in the social media world.'*

Upon moving to Vermont, Tamar wanted to pursue a career in interior design, having dipped her toes into interior design for her friends and family back in Israel. While waiting for new clients, she started to craft and opened her first Etsy shop in 2006. Tamar's style can be described as both romantic and bohemian for the modern woman. Her beautiful jewellery has appeared in numerous books and magazines.

# TAKE GREAT PRODUCT SHOTS

Once you've decided which site(s) you want to use to showcase your crafts, create the best images possible, especially if the site is curated, as you will want to get through the selection process.

Often a varied combination of shots, including both detailed and stylised images, is best. But think about the look and feel of the website you are using to sell your items so your photos fit with its overall feeling. Remember that as people can't touch, try or see your crafts up close and personal, it is imperative to give them as much information as possible through your photographs.

Develop a photo-styling palette. Background and styling don't have to be the same in every image, but they should feel cohesive and they should express your brand. Go for a palette of consistent colours, lighting and props.

If your shop sells several products that are similar in type and scale, use photos to emphasise this. Use your images to represent the different facets of your product. Show specific uses, perspective and colour variations.

Show variations; whether it is multiple photos of the same product in different colours or a single image capturing different styles, product shots are a great way of communicating variation options. Visual clues help customers envision the various ways they can use your products.

When uploading your photos, remember to organise them to appear in a specific order that best tells the story. Always use your best and strongest image first, as this will be the first glimpse your customer gets of your product.

---

**Right:** *Jewellery by Nest Pretty Things (page 68). Tamar's products lend themselves to great photography, which in turn leads to successful listings (page 74).*

# BASIC PHOTOGRAPHY SKILLS

Here's some professional advice from Sussie Bell (www.sussiebell.com), a UK-based freelance location photographer specialising in interiors, crafts and gardens.

## APERTURE

- The top image was shot with a smaller aperture for a sharper image that is fully in focus.

- For the soft focus effect in the image below you should use a wider aperture in order to achieve a more shallow depth of field.

*Standard aperture sizes and camera lenses are shown below. The smaller the aperture number, the wider the aperture, and vice versa.*

f/16    f/11    f/8    f/5.6    f/4    f/2.6

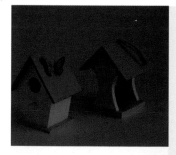

## SHUTTER SPEEDS

- This image is underexposed due to fast shutter speeds. A tripod will help you shoot with slower shutter speeds.

- This image is overexposed due to slower shutter speeds. You will need to adjust these according to light levels.

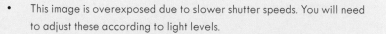

# WORKING WITH LIGHT

- Check the position of your natural light.

- Use white card to reflect the natural light and remove any unwanted shadows.

- The top image was shot next to a natural light source with no reflector.

- The bottom image looks better because it was shot next to the natural light with the use of a reflector to reflect the light back.

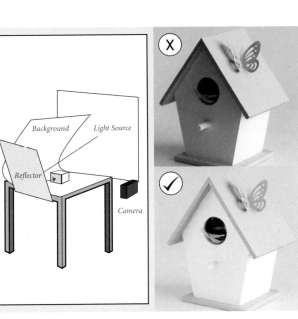

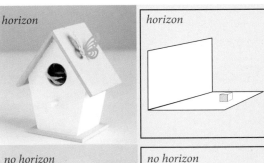

*horizon*

*horizon*

*no horizon*

*no horizon*

# BACKDROPS

- The top image was shot with a background perpendicular to the surface, creating a horizon behind.

- The bottom image was shot with a curved background which eliminates the horizon and gives a better overall effect.

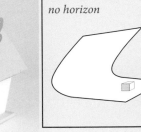

# ANGLE

- The image on the left was shot from the wrong angle and as a result does not do the product justice.

- The image on the right makes the most of the even light and the positioning shows off the product's best features.

# TAKE GREAT CRAFT PRODUCT SHOTS

- Make sure you are familiar with your camera so you can get the best out of it. These days most cameras take good pictures if you know how to make the most of their features. A camera with controllable aperture, shutter speed and flash is preferred but not necessary. Read the camera's manual, even if it is boring!

- If you can afford a tripod, it's a great investment. It's better to work with daylight as opposed to on-camera flash, though you can mix daylight and flash in some situations. On a dull day, you might not be able to hand-hold your camera without the shots coming out blurred, so having the camera fixed on a tripod makes it possible to shoot at slow shutter speeds.

- Choose a bright room in which to do the photography. Put the surface you're working on close to the window to make the most of the light, though you do not want direct sunlight on the product or background. Use a white piece of card on the opposite side to reflect light onto the shadowy side of the product.

- Make sure you place your product on a clean, white surface or at least a plain background. You often need a bigger background than you might think for something small, especially if you are shooting your product from the front. It's ideal if you can curve it up against a wall and place the product as far forward as possible to prevent dark shadows behind it. If the product is flat, lay it on the card and shoot from directly above.

- If you take a light meter reading make sure you take it near the product, as a white background can interfere. This means you might have to overexpose one to two stops to get a well-lit shot.

**Above:** *For best results use a tripod and a curved, white background.*
**Below:** *Reflect natural light back onto the product.*

# WRITE GREAT LISTINGS

After photography, the second most important thing is to tag your crafts well and write excellent listings. Tags are the words that you add to your online images and are the key words people use to search for products. Tweaking these words a little can be really beneficial and help potential customers find your work.

Your tags should include colours, sizes, type of product, and anything else you think a potential customer would like to know. Get a friend or family member to read your descriptions to make sure you have included everything.

Also suggest how your item can be used, if it has multiple applications, and link it with any design trends. This will quickly add lots of keywords to your listings and help with search engine optimisation (SEO).

If you offer bespoke options, be sure to include this information or a link to another listing where you already have these options laid out.

*'Keep it simple and as accurate as possible, always write measurements, and think like a buyer. What kind of info would you like to get from this listing before buying it?'*
Tamar Schechner, Nest Pretty Things

Try to make sure you fit in with traditional gifting times like Mother's Day or Christmas. This will ensure you get more sales throughout the year.

Bring your crafts to life by sharing thoughts about how and why you created them. Creating a sense of rareness also adds value.

To improve your credibility and positioning, it really helps if you are able to group your products into a collection or theme. That way your products will be displayed together and will look far stronger and more professional than a random mix of products. On the right is an example of a great listing from Tamar's Etsy page – it is clear, detailed and informative.

**Colourful Chunky Bead Strand Necklace**

## £17.98 GBP
**Only 1 available**

**Overview**
- Handmade
- Materials: glass, brass
- Feedback: 5108 reviews
- Ships worldwide

Choose ONE long necklace (the matt gold beads are now available in a matt silver option!)

1. 8mm Czech glass beads in gold, orange and aqua.

2. Smoky lilac and centre 10mm jet black bead with 8mm Swarovski creamy glass pearls on the ends.

3. 8mm Czech glass beads in aqua, gold and red.

4. 8mm Czech glass beads in gold and mint, two beads in pink and the middle bead 10mm is beige.

5. A centre 10mm jet black bead with 8mm beads in gold and Swarovski creamy glass pearls.

6. 8mm Czech glass beads in gold, chartreuse and pale aqua.

The colours are perfect for any season; wear it with your favourite winter jumper or a breezy summer outfit.

The chain is a chunky super high-quality lead- and nickel-free antiqued brass made in the USA that connects seamlessly to the draped beaded part and sits beautifully around your neck.

Please note the chain for the 28"–34" will be a thinner antique brass chain more suitable for longer lengths. Check it out here: https://www.etsy.com/listing/82672819

Shipped wrapped in an eco-friendly gift box.

# MEET THE CRAFTERS
## MEL STRINGER

Mel Stringer, of Brisbane, Australia, is the creator of unique papercraft company Girlie Pains. The daughter of a cartoonist, she has been drawing since she was little, and now sells her downloadable papercraft pdfs, accompanied by detailed listings, on her Etsy site. Mel also currently writes a blog, illustrates for *Frankie* magazine, and works as a freelance commercial artist for many global clients.

*'Be creative, informative and organised with your specifications. Keep on top of it!'*

# CUSTOMER SERVICE

Customer service starts with the basics. It is essential that you communicate clearly with your customers even before they become your customers. Being on a well-known site will help your customers feel more secure, but having a shop that feels welcoming will put them at ease. Having great images, accurate descriptions, a personal profile or 'about' page, and a feedback page will help them establish a personal connection with you and will contribute to your positive professionalism and credibility.

Communication is paramount. Be clear and upfront about your postage costs and maintain solid contact throughout the transaction. That way you can prevent confusion and build rapport.

When someone orders from you, promptly send them a friendly message thanking them and acknowledging their order.

Be clear with your customers what your returns policy is. (If you don't have a returns policy yet, you need to make one. Make sure you consider various options in order to find the right policy for you.)

Honesty is the best policy. Be upfront and honest in your communication with your potential customers. If you post only on weekends or are on holiday for a week, let them know. They will appreciate it!

*'I like my products to be received to look as if they are a wrapped present.'*
Vicky Trainor

Everyone encounters bumps in the road when setting up their own business. Think about how you will handle dissatisfied customers, and always remain professional and graceful in your dealing with any situation that might arise. Most importantly, stay positive and keep things in perspective as there will always be a solution.

Instead of placing blame, think about what you can do to make it right. Start by acknowledging the issue and taking practical steps to resolve it. Look at the problem from your customer's viewpoint, so he or she feels heard. More often than not, once you understand the customer's point of view, you can fix the problem.

Remember, as a small business owner, you rely on positive feedback. It really isn't worth your energy to get into an argument with one customer over money. Sometimes it is worth braving the loss for the sake of your long-term gain.

Try to learn from your mistakes by refining your production process and making your packaging more robust and protective. See each sale that goes awry as a learning experience. Remember, one of the great things about selling online is that when you get too stressed you can walk away, breathe, compose yourself and then deal with the issue.

## TIPS

- Provide excellent customer service before, during and after the transaction. Small personal gestures like adding a voucher code, a free gift or a handwritten note can encourage your buyers to come back for more as these touches distinguish you from big retailers and establish a special connection with you and your brand.

- Think of the way you communicate with your customers as an extension of your brand. If your shop could talk, what would it say? Would it be playful, sweet or formal? You want your customers to walk away feeling good, no matter what, so with every transaction, it is worth thinking about how your response will complement your brand.

**Below, left and right:**
*Good customer service can be achieved through small touches such as pretty packaging.*

# HOW TO PRICE YOUR CRAFTS

To have a successful craft business, you need to make money, and to make money you need to figure out how to sell your crafts to make a profit.

To survive and thrive in the business, you must approach pricing from a businesslike perspective. Putting a price tag on your work is one of the most difficult tasks of setting up any business. It requires you to establish a monetary value on very subjective qualities like style, experience and care.

As a general business rule, you should price your crafts high enough to cover your costs and make some profit without going beyond what your customers are willing to pay. Pricing depends on your selling goals. If you're not too concerned about making a profit, you can estimate prices more loosely.

Start with estimating target prices by going over some calculations based on the information below and then researching the market, identifying similar products in the marketplace where you will be selling, whether it's online or in local craft fairs and retail outlets.

There are lots of pricing techniques, but most follow a common methodology using formulas to make initial estimates, then refining those estimates based on practical factors and savvy guesses. Over time you can use your bookkeeping records to track how well your goods sell at which prices and adjust prices accordingly. You can also look at streamlining your prices by buying supplies wholesale and improving your workflow in order to turn around a bigger profit.

# TIPS

- Always write down the expenses you incur, so you can adjust your prices accordingly over time.

- Don't take the easy way out by slashing your prices and assuming you will sell more. Unique handmade products command higher prices everywhere; people associate low prices with cheaply made items.

- Know the community where you will be selling your work. If you are selling your goods in person at a local craft fair or an upscale boutique, get to know the community and window-shop your competition's pricing as well.

- Educate your customers. More often than not, your customers are totally unaware of the time you have spent on your craft or your attention to detail. Helping them understand can reassure them that your pricing is right.

- Engage with your customers. The wealth of information you can glean from them can be very insightful. They often know nothing about you and what you do, so they will often have a different opinion than someone who knows you or your product well.

- Can you do any cost cutting? Get creative and see how you can alter the design to produce the work in multiples, reducing the labour. Look around and see if you can buy your materials with a bulk discount.

- Improve the perceived value of your item by improving or enhancing any number of its core elements, like the packaging or your reputation.

- Prices don't have to be stagnant. If you feel you are not gaining a fair income or your pieces are just not moving fast enough, change your approach.

Here's the approach we will be using: use a pricing formula to estimate a 'working' wholesale price range. Use the working wholesale price range to estimate a retail price range.

There are always two types of costs relevant to pricing: direct costs and indirect costs. Direct costs are the unique costs of making a finished product. They include the cost of raw materials and labour. Indirect costs are the same as overhead costs, which are general expenses that you incur no matter what finished goods you make. Once you quantify all these costs, you can plug them into pricing formulas.

## FORMULA

Materials + Labour + Expenses + Profit = Wholesale

Wholesale x 2 = Retail

## EXAMPLE

Materials (£1) + Labour (£2) = £3 (direct costs)

+ Expenses (£1) (indirect cost)

+ Profit (£2) = Wholesale Price (£6)

Wholesale x 2 = £12 (Retail Price)

Gross profit = £6

# THINGS TO CONSIDER

 ## MATERIALS

- Determine your total cost of raw material components by making a list of all the materials you used to create the product (based on average cost per unit). This will include small stuff like thread, paint, glitter, and other items that may have cost you only pennies. Don't forget to include the cost of postage if you ordered supplies online.

 ## LABOUR

- Estimate how long it takes to make one item. Calculate how many items you can produce in one hour. Decide how much money you wish to earn per hour of creating crafts and what your time is worth to you. Multiply your hourly rate by the time it takes to make one product.

 ## EXPENSES

- To get accurate overhead costs, you will need to work out your office expenses and monthly expenses and combine these to get your general overhead expenses.

- Office expenses include the costs for items such as your packaging, branded stationery, promotional material and postage. Don't forget expenses like your sellers' fees or craft show set-up costs. Divide your total overhead costs by the number of items you are selling.

- Your monthly expenses are rent, electricity, phone, water, etc. — expenses generally paid on a monthly basis. The easiest way to figure out these expenses is by dividing the total monthly expense by the number of hours in a month in order to calculate an hourly rate. Then multiply this by how many hours in a month you spend producing your craft item.

## PROFIT

- At this point you need to consider where you want your craft business to go and how much your market can bear. Only you can decide, based on the crafts you are selling and the skill involved, what figure you insert here. But please be good to yourself and your craft.

## WHOLESALE AND RETAIL PRICE

- Now, add up your figures for materials, labour, expenses and profit. This will give you a wholesale price range.

- Multiply your wholesale price by two to estimate a retail price range (Wholesale Price x 2 = Retail Price).

## MEET THE CRAFTERS
### WHITNEY SMITH

Whitney Smith is the creator of Whitney Smith Pottery. Whitney fell in love with throwing clay on the wheel when she took a class at Cabrillo College in Santa Cruz, California, in 1994. She went on to the University of California to study for a degree in anthropology, but continued to work in her garage studio and assisted another Santa Cruz artist, Sandi Dihl, at her clay studio.

*'If you are very good at what you do, you will have a perfect business every once in a while for about thirty-six hours. If you are very blessed, you won't lose your mind for the rest of the time when it's not.'*

While she seriously considered going on to graduate studies for anthropology, she felt a deep passion for clay, which she wanted to turn into a full-time living. After relocating to California's Bay Area, she worked as a floral designer and as an assistant for potter Bob Pool while continuing to develop her own pots on the side. With the help and support of family, friends and customers, she was able to make the leap to full-time ceramic artist in early 2000.

# PAYMENT PROCESSING

When you first start your craft business, you need to think about how you are going to accept payment for your products. You never want to miss a sale because you lack the accepted payment methods.

If you are going to sell your crafts online, I would suggest signing up for a PayPal account, so you can start accepting credit and debit card payments instantly. As there are no set-up fees, it can be a good way to get started. Familiarise yourself with how PayPal works and be sure to read all the guidelines and advice they give.

Prior to selling your crafts in person, for example at a craft fair, be sure you have enough cash (both notes and change) to make change for a cash sale.

New technology and apps that transform your smartphone or tablet into a mobile point-of-sale terminal that accepts credit card payments are appearing all the time. Being able to conveniently sell products at a moment's notice using the smartphone you already have isn't the only benefit; often customers are willing to spend more when they know they can use their credit card, so it's worth doing some research.

# POSTAGE

Postage is an integral part of selling online, as it is the method by which your customers receive your goods. You need to start by laying solid groundwork for postage methods, so you can send your packages with confidence. Start by researching the packaging options available to you.

## TIPS

- Buy a digital scale that measures kilograms as well as grams and weigh each item with all of the wrapping and packaging prior to listing. If you sell many of the same items, you won't have to weigh each time.

- Use a postage calculator, which can be found on your country's postal website, for all your national and international packages.

- For international packages, always include a customs form on the outside and an invoice with pricing and the mailing address of your recipient inside the package.

- If you can, try to offer flat-rate postage. This is easier to do if you sell smaller items. It allows shoppers to purchase multiple items from you, knowing that there will be a maximum cost limit.

- Consider charging a handling charge if you sell high-quality items and if you package them as if they are special gifts for each and every customer.

- If you have made a mistake and overcharged on the postage, refund the difference to your customer. Your customer will always appreciate a refund.

- Save your postage receipt until you know the package has arrived, and obtain a tracking number and email it to the customer so they can follow the progress of their goods online.

# PACKAGING

When you sell your products online, you need to pay special attention to packing your items for safe postage, but you also want the packaging to look professional. The way you package your products says something about you and your brand. Your packaging is part of your branding, so let it reflect your style through the colours, material and pattern you use.

Of course, I don't need to tell you that you must take steps to ensure that your item arrives in one piece, so careful consideration needs to go into its transit. With some careful thought and research into protective packaging, you can find a way to post almost anything safely and securely. Use cushioning materials like shredded paper or bubble wrap to prevent breakage, and plenty of sturdy packaging tape to ensure your package doesn't fall apart en route. For bendable crafts, such as artwork and prints, back them with firm cardboard. Don't be excessive with your packaging though and do consider using recycled materials. Remember, the first thing your customer will see of your actual work is the packaging, so strive to delight him or her with great original packaging that reflects your brand, as it will leave a lasting first impression which is likely to secure you further sales.

*Great packaging is essential. Without overpackaging your items, find a way to make your customers feel special. If you offer gift wrapping as standard, make sure you cover your costs in your item price; otherwise, offer it as a separate service.*

*Wrap as you would want to receive the item yourself. The first view of your product that the customer sees is your packaging, so whether they spend a small or a considerable amount, it is important that the good service remains consistent.*

# LINO BLOCK RUBBER STAMP

Stamping is easy and quick, but to make something totally handmade and unique, design your own rubber stamp. Then, use your stamps to customise your packing box.

*1.* The first thing to do is create your design. Once you are happy with the design, transfer it to the linoleum block. There are a couple of ways to do this.

- If your design is on the computer, print it out in black and white using an inkjet printer. Trim your design to size and place it face down on the block. Gently rub the back of the paper with vinegar, making sure you keep your paper in one place. OR
- Use a pencil to draw the outline of your design onto tracing paper. Place the image face down on the linoleum block and rub with a coin to transfer the pencil drawing from the paper to the block.

*2.* Use the pencil to clearly define the area you wish to carve and then with the finest blade you have, carve all of the dark area or the area that you don't want to hold ink. It helps to carve around the image first to give yourself a good solid border within which to work.

*3.* Ink the block with the stamp pad.

*4.* Set the block down onto a piece of scrap paper and ensure the image is showing up the right way. If not, tweak your carving to make it exactly right. If there are edges that seem to be picking up ink, let the ink dry and then carve them down to a reasonable level.

## TOOLS & MATERIALS

- Linoleum (or Speedy-Carve™) block
- Inkjet printer, paper and vinegar OR tracing paper, pencil and coin
- Linoleum carving knife
- Stamp pad

1

2

## TIP

- Choose a design which features throughout all your branding as well as your workspace.

# HOW TO MAKE...

## DECORATIVE PAPER BOW

A decorative paper bow adds a special touch to your packaging. You can use any type of pretty paper to suit your brand and finish with a small button or cabochon for extra flair.

*1.* Photocopy the bow templates below, use the photocopier again to enlarge them to the required size and then cut out.

*2.* Trace templates on to your paper, then cut out.

*3.* Apply double-sided tape to the centre of the 'loops' piece and bend in the two outer edges to the centre. Press the ends down on to the tape to adhere.

*4.* Apply tape to the centre of the 'loops' piece and press it on to the 'bow ends' piece.

*5.* Decorate centre with a small button or cabochon if desired.

### TOOLS & MATERIALS
- Photocopy of template below
- Pencil
- Scissors
- Pretty paper
- Double-sided tape
- Small button or cabochon (optional)

### TIP
- Why not print your own pretty paper with a linoleum-cut stamp (page 87)?

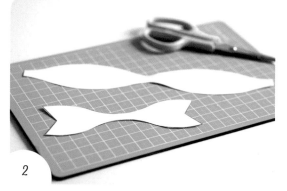

2

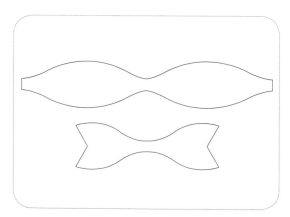

3

# CHAPTER 4

# SELLING
# IN PERSON

Even if you have a successful online shop, selling in person can help your crafts reach new or different customers. You can start with low-pressure, community-sponsored events and even work up to selling your crafts in shops.

- Selling your crafts in person (page 92)

- Setting up your stall (page 93)

- Selling skills (page 96)

- Displaying your crafts (page 98)

- After the event (page 104)

- Selling in shops (page 106)

# SELLING YOUR CRAFTS IN PERSON

Don't limit yourself to selling online. The easiest way to start selling in person is to put on a craft show at home. Invite a few close friends and family members, asking them to bring friends who have expressed interest in your craft. Keep the show very casual and provide light refreshments. You could pick a theme for your event and tie it in with the seasons; the obvious one being Christmas when the interest and demand for handmade crafts is always high. Community-sponsored events are another great way to start selling in person. Ask friends and family if they know of any upcoming events where you could sell your crafts.

Craft fairs are an obvious selling venue. You might want to visit a few so you can see the range of work and quality sold by others. This is also a great opportunity to speak to exhibitors and decide which are the best types of fairs for you and your products. Consider the number of visitors attending the fair, the costs involved in setting up your stall, and how many goods you will need to sell to make a profit.

Start with a small fair where the cost of a table will be lower. This gives you a great opportunity to obtain useful feedback. Choosing a local fair will also mean minimal travel costs and you can ask your friends and family to support you. If the fair you would like to attend is very popular, schedule a meeting with the organiser to find out what they want from an exhibitor. Some will ask to see examples of your work, so put your best photos and products forward! Remember, stall spaces at many events get fully booked in advance.

# SETTING UP YOUR STALL

Think of your craft fair, booth or stall as your flagship store; a portable retail outlet representing you and your brand. It is your opportunity to stand out from the crowd and to invite people to experience and connect with your brand. The more work you put into it, the better its impact, which in turn will make you more memorable, and will help you sell your products and gain a following. The more creative you are with your space, the better your chances of engaging customers.

You want customers to look for your booth with anticipation and excitement.

Start by browsing other craft show stands for inspiration. You can do this online by visiting photography sites such as Flickr (page 123), which contain groups dedicated to craft stalls and booths, and by personally visiting craft shows. Write notes on what you like and don't like about the displays and refer to these when creating your own stall.

# THINGS TO CONSIDER

### ( 1 ) COLOUR

Colours should enhance the presentation, not compete against the crafts for attention. You don't want your items to be washed out by colours or patterns that are too bold or busy, so choose colours that make your products shine. Think about adding a complementary design on the floor or a colour scheme to the ceiling to tie the space together. Consistency in theme and colour is necessary if you want a positive emotional response from customers as well as the ability to make yourself easily remembered and recognised. Keep your theme and brand in mind when choosing colours. Think about the ambience created by different colours and consider the feel of the show so your stand makes sense. For instance, for a Christmas show, you will want to evoke a warm, festive spirit.

### ( 2 ) LEVELS

Stools and small cabinets provide additional multidimensional levels and can also help direct traffic through your booth or stall. Creating levels diversifies the visual presentation, stops the booth from looking overcrowded, and increases the space in which to display items while at the same time reducing traffic jams around tables.

1    *Think about the mood you want to create when people visit your stand.*

2    *Create height on your table and remember to display your pieces where people can reach out and touch them.*

**3** *Everything in your stand should be clearly priced, labelled and identified for the customer.*

 SIGNAGE

Signage can help engage the customer and is important to help make the visitor feel informed. Without the basic information about the product, the materials and the cost, the customer may walk away rather than ask for help. Prominently display your logo and have business cards and other promotional materials easily available to remind visitors who you are and what your brand is all about. (Be careful not to overdo it though, as you still want them to see your crafts.)

**4** PROMOTION

Promote your show online and 'practise' what your table will look like when it's set up. Take photos and use them to promote your upcoming show.

**4** *Practise setting up your stall and take attractive photographs to display on your website to promote an upcoming event.*

# SELLING SKILLS

Give people a bit of space. Don't pounce on them as soon as they stop by your stall. However, you should stop chatting with your partner/helper when a customer enters your booth or starts looking at your table, as you won't get another chance to sell to him or her.

Wait for someone to pick up something or inspect a price tag, then you can open a dialogue by telling them useful information about the product or price.

Be friendly. Nobody wants to visit a stall where someone looks grumpy and unwelcoming. It's basic, but a smile makes all the difference. Don't be offended if someone doesn't want to converse with you. Remember, some people are just rude, and there's nothing you can do but remain polite and forget about it.

Even the biggest craft makers have days when they don't sell anything. It can be heartbreaking, but sometimes it's more to do with the advertising for the event, the weather, or maybe just that the stars aren't aligned.

If you are trading outdoors, check the weather forecast the night before, as there is nothing worse than freezing with no jacket, or wearing warm boots on a hot day.

Take some crafts with you so when it is quiet you can finish up a bit of hand sewing or finally knit the last rows on that scarf you have been meaning to finish for ages. This has the added benefit of letting your potential customers know that the items are made by you. It is also a great conversation starter.

Include links to all your social media and Internet shopfronts on all the marketing material that you hand out at craft fairs. Shoppers who don't buy on the day of the event are likely to visit your website later when they are ready to shop.

## MEET THE CRAFTERS
### VICKY TRAINOR

Vicky Trainor is the creator of handmade homeware brands The Vintage Drawer and The Linen Garden. Vicky has been a crafter since she can remember, always collecting, gathering, investigating and making.

*'I do love to trial products at fairs and to be able to discuss with people what they think about certain designs, products and prices. It is also so rewarding to meet people as "real people" in "real life".'*

This led her down the path of studying textiles and embroidery at college. Her current project, The Vintage Drawer, involves gathering and doing everything she loves: textiles, embroidery, design, decoration, fabrics, treasured possessions and haberdashery, as well as making, hoarding, recycling, reclaiming, styling, and then applying the 'make, do and mend' ethos. She mainly works with damaged embroidered table linens and vintage fabrics mixed with brand new cotton ones.

# DISPLAYING YOUR CRAFTS

Creating small groups of designs and showing only one piece per design keeps your booth looking minimal, but enables you to show a lot of merchandise.

Keep it subtle. Your displays should never compete with your product; they are there to complement and make your product stand out. Even if you come up with the most beautiful, elaborate display in the world, it's of no use if people spend all their time admiring your display and don't even notice your products.

When buying display props, consider how you would be able to use them in your home. That way your items will be multifunctional and not a wasted expense if your first craft show isn't as profitable as you had hoped. For instance, you can use old bookshelves covered with

wallpaper to make an eye-catching booth display. The shelves can always be put to use in your home.

Make sure you take enough stock; it is always better to have too much than not enough. Consider how long the fair will last. Is it being held in the evening, afternoon, all day, on a weekday, weekend, or near Christmas? Think about how big your stand will be and how many products you will need to fill it. Making more of your smaller, more inexpensive items may pay off at smaller events where people carry less cash but may impulse buy with what they have. Be cautious and make more products than you think you will need; you can always use the extra for your next fair or your online shop.

Keep your stand neat and tidy to evoke the message that you, the exhibitor, are a professional. Clutter does not help develop a sense of quality or tastefulness. There are several ways to create the feeling of abundance without the clutter. First, try to group craft products – like with like items. For example, if you have handmade magnets, you might want to consider placing them on a magnetic board affixed to the wall. Once the supply diminishes, add more magnets. When you are running low, use your remaining magnets to hang promotional material.

Some craft fairs do not assign specific locations, so it is well worth getting to the venue early to choose a good spot. This also gives you time to park your vehicle and get organised, so as soon as the first person comes through the door you are ready.

Find out in advance if you need liability insurance to sell at the craft fair and research accordingly.

*'Always mock up your stall beforehand, find ways to give your stall height or even a backdrop, and try to present your goods in the way they would be used by your customers. Don't just pile everything on your tabletop and hope for the best! Above all, make it pretty! Use props that show off your items to their best (often charity shops and vintage shops are the best source for ideas) and be sure to choose objects that fit in well with your brand.'*
Emma Lamb

## DISPLAY YOUR CRAFTS

Hangers can be used to hang not only clothing but accessories such as scarves and belts, and interior decorations like pillowcases, blankets and quilts. Why not make your hangers fit in with the feel and look of your brand by covering them in fabric or paint?

## Brand hangers

*1.* Start by laying strips of double-sided tape onto your scraps of fabric. Carefully cut out your strips of fabric along the edge of the tape so your fabric strips are entirely covered by the tape.

*2.* Peel back about an inch of the backing tape and attach the end of the tape to the hanger. Wrap the strip tightly around the hanger, tape side down, continuing to peel back the tape as you wrap. Continue wrapping tightly until you run out of fabric. Start up again with the next fabric strip, always concealing the end of the previous strip.

*3.* When you get back around to where you started, wrap the strip around the hook of the hanger. Trim off any long loose ends and tie a bow with ribbon at neck.

### TOOLS & MATERIALS
- Double-sided tape
- Fabric scraps
- Wire hangers
- Ribbon

## Painted hangers

*1.* Cover the hanger's metal hook with masking tape, so it doesn't get covered in spray paint.

*2.* Following the instructions on the spray paint, carefully spray the wooden hanger until you have an even coat of paint and the original colour of the hanger is no longer visible.

*3.* Allow to dry. I prefer to do several light coats so the paint does not drip and I get an even coat.

### TOOLS & MATERIALS
- Wooden hangers
- Masking tape
- Spray paint suitable for wood

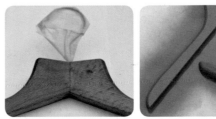

# CRAFT FAIR CHECKLIST

### 1 DISPLAY SUPPLIES
- ☐ Inventory
- ☐ Displays
- ☐ Signage
- ☐ Power strip/extension leads and lights (check beforehand that you will have a connection and if they charge)
- ☐ Rolling trolleys, bags
- ☐ Emergency kit – safety pins, bungee cord, cable ties, scissors, string, twine tape
- ☐ Plastic or covering in case of rain

### 2 MAKING SALES
- ☐ Change
- ☐ Credit payment system (try square.com, or look at options with your mobile phone, as suggested on page 82)
- ☐ Receipt or sales book
- ☐ Packaging materials, boxes, gift wrap, tags
- ☐ Pens

### 3 MARKETING SUPPLIES
- ☐ Business cards
- ☐ Other promotional materials
- ☐ Mailing list signup sheet

### 4 PERSONAL SUPPLIES
- ☐ Cash apron or bag
- ☐ Personal emergency kit – tissues, lip balm, sunscreen, aspirin, plasters
- ☐ Water and snacks
- ☐ Chair
- ☐ Craft supplies
- ☐ Extra clothes to keep you warm, sunhat to shade you from the sun, or raincoat
- ☐ Comfortable shoes

# AFTER THE EVENT

After each craft fair, calculate how much profit you have made, taking into account the fee for the event, travel costs, and any miscellaneous costs you hadn't considered.

By finding out which products earned you the most money, you can adjust your production accordingly.

It is also worth considering how many sales you made as a result of your marketing efforts at each fair. If you get only one regular customer by being at a fair – maybe it's a customer who only picked up your business card at the fair and later visited your website – that fair helped your business grow.

With experience, you will be able to decide which fairs are the most profitable for you to attend, so you can schedule them into your calendar.

*'I always ensure I have leaflets at a fair for both avenues of my business. Everyone who visits my stall, whether for a chat or to browse or to purchase, will leave with a pretty collection of leaflets. I try to make my leaflets visually interesting, hoping that people will simply want to keep them because they like looking at them. Some even use them on their pin boards back in their own studios.'*

Vicky Trainor,
The Vintage Drawer

# SELLING IN SHOPS

Selling your crafts in shops is a great way to expand your business. There is also a certain prestige attached to showing your work in shops. Before you even think about approaching a shop, however, make sure you have a wide variety of products, your branding, presentation, packaging and pricing determined, and your website or social media up and running.

Now for the golden question. How do you get your products in the shop? There is no guaranteed way of doing this, but follow some basic steps, check out the mistakes to avoid, and you'll be well on your way to selling in shops.

Start by looking around your local and neighbouring towns for potential shops for your crafts. Make sure they are in different areas and are not in direct competition with each other.

It is of paramount importance that you personally visit the shops you are hoping to sell to. Resist introducing yourself on this visit. Just look around and observe how they sell, package and promote their goods. Check their prices and look for similar items to yours, so you can be sure the quality and style of your crafts fit with what they already sell. Follow up your research by going online and checking out their websites and social media. Really get to know the shops you plan to approach before approaching them.

Once you've decided on the list of potential shops, contact the manager, owner or buyer by telephone or email to schedule a meeting. Think of your meeting as if you are at a job interview and always remain courteous, professional and confident about your products and brand. Always take samples to your meetings. Your product should be branded well, with some nice packaging to make it look complete.

Work out your wholesale prices in advance (see the formula explained on pages 78–80), as this is what the shop will pay you. You can sell your items online for your retail price, but you must accept that shops need to make money to cover overheads such as rent, insurance and staff, and so they need to make a profit too. The buyer will also want to know your suggested retail

## WHAT NOT TO DO

- Turn up unannounced with your goods and start pitching them to the owner. Most shop owners will find this really inconsiderate and intrusive.

- Have flimsy prices. Make sure you know your wholesale pricing. Do not expect your potential buyer to do this for you.

- Be pushy.

- Talk only about yourself and your products. Try engaging the buyer in conversation about their store and what you love about it. After all, everyone likes to be flattered.

- Beat yourself up if the buyer turns you down. There are hundreds of reasons why they might not take your products, including pricing issues, space, or similarity to items they already sell.

price. Work out your terms and conditions before your meeting. 'Terms' describes how and when you accept payment. 'Conditions' refers to things like minimum opening order, such as the shop must take a minimum of 10 items or an order of no less than £75, and what, if any, discounts you can give if they take more.

Finally, spend some time putting together a fact sheet, brochure or at least a business card to leave with the seller. It should include your contact information, your terms and conditions, wholesale and recommended retail prices. It could also include beautiful photographs and enticing descriptions of your products which will leave a lasting impression with the shop owner. Not only will this give you more confidence during your meeting, but it will also strengthen your position as a professional.

# MEET THE CRAFTERS
## ANNE CRESCI

Anne Cresci is the creator of Matilou, an illustrated goods brand. After studying graphic design and fine arts at L' école Emile Cohl in Lyon, France, she began professionally illustrating in 1999 and ten years later discovered Etsy. Work was quite slow at that time and she wanted to try something new, so she started making jewellery based on her illustrations.

*'I often feel guilty about the mess when customers come to my shop. But I think they like the "messy artistic" look… which is a very good excuse for my weakness.'*

Inspired by all the crafters she met, Anne started a collection of new illustrations just for herself, to inspire her necklaces. From there her business really grew and now she owns a cute little boutique called Matilou in Lyon, where she lives with her two children, Matis and Lou.

# CHAPTER 5

# MARKETING

Having started up their craft business, many individuals make the mistake of not investing enough time in promoting themselves and their crafts. You have to put yourself out there in a way that clearly reflects who you are, what you do and why it matters. Everything you do should be a professional reflection of your brand; always put your best foot forward. Knowing how to market your crafts and yourself is one of the most important things any crafter must learn.

# SPREADING THE WORD

**M**arketing, in a nutshell, is exposing and explaining your brand or product to your chosen marketplace in order to sell it. No matter how beautiful your crafts are and how unique your brand is, if you don't market them, you will never be able to make any sort of profit. No one can buy your product if they don't know about it.

Marketing takes a lot of hard work and patience and you need to do it as an ongoing activity for the life of your business. Huge corporations plough large sums of money into marketing their companies and products and, whether we like it or not, we know it works. However, when it comes to marketing you and your brand, there are lots of methods that don't cost anything.

Networking, which I prefer to call 'making friends with like-minded creatives', is simply being visible in your community.

> *'We always carry business cards with us, you never know when you might get the opportunity to hand one out!'*
> City Chic Country Mouse

It's about meeting new people both in person and online in a friendly and genuine way. It will help you build a network of friends and business associates who help strengthen your understanding of the craft industry. I have met some wonderful friends at blogging events, craft shows and through my social networks. So get out there and say 'Hello!'; if there is one thing that can be said about crafters, it is that they are genuine, lovely people!

## TIPS

- Give out business cards. Collect them too, as it is a great way of following up with people you meet.

- Pick the networking techniques that fit best with your personality and style.

- Start conversations with like-minded crafters on your social network sites.

- Don't leave networking to chance; look for trade or industry events like fairs, exhibitions and showcases, and attend whenever you can.

- Think of networking as a way to help other people.

- Smile and enjoy yourself. It is supposed to be fun, not a chore. Just be yourself!

- If you take on employees, even part-time, you'll need to familiarise yourself with employment laws and know how to get the best out of your staff.

# DEVELOPING MARKETING MATERIALS

Before you start developing marketing materials, you need to think about the benefits of your product. What is it about your product that differentiates it from the competition? Compile a list of the unique selling points.

Put together a nice catalogue or brochure of the different crafts that you want to market. As always, make sure your photographs are the best they can be and are high-resolution. Make sure your descriptions are clear so that people can read through your brochure or catalogue and get a clear sense of your crafts. It is a good idea to make a separate price list that you can update regularly according to the size of any order you get.

Use every means of promotion available. Do not just rely on your virtual shop or craft stall to attract new customers and awareness of your brand. Create your own blog and capitalise on the strength of established sites such as Facebook, Twitter, Flickr and Pinterest to promote your brand. Spreading the word happens when people believe in and love your brand and promote it to their own audiences through discussion, content and sharing. Start networking with magazines and other blogs to let them know about you and your brand and inform them of any new or exciting things you have in the pipeline.

## TIPS

- Create both virtual and printed marketing materials in order to reach as many people as possible.

- Stand out from the crowd by being as bold and inventive as possible in your approach.

# PROMOTE YOURSELF ONLINE

It's a well-known fact that Internet users watch less television. Who can blame them when there are lovely blogs to read, loads of wonderful inspiration to see on Pinterest, friends to catch up with on Facebook, and online learning. If I am not decorating my house, making crafts, eating, sleeping and working, you can bet your bottom dollar I am whiling away the hours on the Internet. Think about the huge audience on the web to whom you can introduce your lovely crafts. Get your pictures and web links out there, but don't overtly sell your crafts, unless on an official selling site, as it can look unprofessional. Be part of a community and contribute without expecting something in return.

Where do you start? There is a wealth of social websites to which you can contribute and a whole heap of opportunities. Why not start using one or two, and once you have started to develop a following, branch out from there. Most of the social media services are free, so you can sign up for all of them (remember to use your brand name) and then try them out to see which ones you like the best.

*Left and below: Promoting yourself online is simple in an age of popular social media websites.*

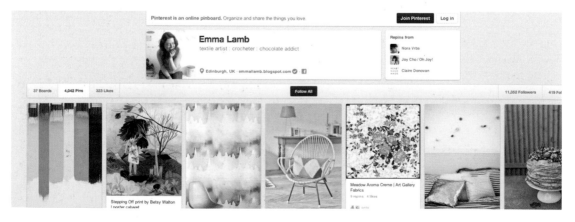

Tabitha Emma Bray, the creator of embroidered craft brand Tabitha Emma, is an Australian designer and crafter. She learned to sew in high school where a class project making coin purses really left its mark. Later, Tabitha Emma trained in Fashion and Textile Design at the Whitehouse Institute of Design and studied graphic design and communication at Enmore Design Centre, Tafe.

*'Twitter is my favourite social media platform. It's been a great way to find out about design and craft events and to keep in touch with like-minded people who appreciate what you do.'*

Tabitha began selling on Etsy in 2007 after deciding the fashion industry wasn't for her. Selling her handmade bags and purses online, her business quickly grew and has since been expanding into different fields with the help of lots of inspiring people who have encouraged and spurred her on.

Tabitha loves to create and design, working in a wide range of creative fields including illustration, textiles, fashion, print graphics, digital animation and web design. She has been freelancing full-time since the beginning of 2010, and part-time since 2007.

# FACEBOOK

Facebook is the world's leading social networking platform in use today, both in terms of outreach and number of users. But as a small craft business, how do you make the most of it?

Beyond personal networking, Facebook can be a powerful tool for your craft brand. It offers many ways to promote your business to its online community, from creating a Facebook page for your business and starting a topical group, to launching a targeted ad campaign. A Facebook presence should be on everyone's list of must-haves for social marketing. Your friends and family may want to see pictures of your kids posted on Facebook, but unless you're a portrait photographer, your customers probably don't. So having a Facebook page is the best way to separate your personal life and your business; beyond that, a page has built-in tools and features that enable you to interact with your network uniquely. For instance, only Facebook users with a page can buy and post Facebook ads and use the Facebook 'insights', which lets you see which posts are working and which aren't. Figure out how to make something go viral and gain insight into the demographics of your page's followers.

But what exactly is a Facebook page? In the words of Facebook: 'A Facebook page is a public profile that enables you to share your business and products with Facebook users.' Anyone with a Facebook account can create a Facebook page within minutes, and it's free and easy. However, creating a Facebook page, and creating a great Facebook page that engages your readers, are two very different things. Fortunately, the good news is that you don't have to be a web designer, programmer, marketing expert or technology guru to create an irresistible and engaging Facebook page. All you need is a little patience, time and some good advice (which, of course, you will find here).

Let's start with the basics of creating a Facebook page. If you are not already signed up on Facebook, you will need to do so first with a personal account. Once you have logged onto your personal page, go to the Facebook 'Create a Page' site. As a crafter you will want a 'Brand or Product' page unless you have a local business shopfront. Fill in the brand name, click 'Get Started', and your page is created. Yes, it is that easy!

Remember to choose a great username. I would strongly advise that you use your craft brand name as your username as it will also appear in the URL (web address) for your page. There are already a lot of Facebook pages, so your first choice might not be available. That's why it's critical that you create a Facebook page and claim your username as soon as possible. Even if you don't plan to rely heavily on Facebook today, you might want to in the future.

*'My blog and Facebook page are my favourite places to self-promote, talk about my work and connect with my customers. They are the two places where I feel I can talk about my work endlessly without getting that guilty feeling of overdoing it! My blog is perfect for more in-depth introductions to new work as I can show lots of images in one post and get across all the information I want to, while my Facebook page has a larger audience and is great for quick updates and reminders.'*

Emma Lamb

Get acquainted with the Facebook page rules, found on the 'Learn More' pages, so you make sure you do not break any of the rules, which could result in your page being closed before you have even started! The next thing you'll want to do is add a profile picture. This is the smaller image that appears on your Facebook page and then as your avatar on all posts and photos you publish on Facebook. I would recommend using your brand logo as the profile photo for your Facebook page, because the more that people see it, the more they'll recognise it and associate it with your brand.

## ADDITIONAL FEATURES

You will also need to add a Timeline cover photo that is a strong representation of your brand so visitors immediately know what to expect from you. A great photo that showcases your crafts and captures people's attention would be ideal. The Timeline is a new Facebook design function that merges both the Facebook wall and profile into one page, creating a better viewing experience of all the past and present content on your Facebook page.

Your Facebook page includes a small 'About' section, where you can include a couple of sentences about your craft business. Make sure you include the most important information about what you offer to your audience so they instantly understand why your page should matter to them. Keep your writing succinct and keyword-rich as this area is used in searches; choose your keywords carefully.

Also, it is extremely important that you include your website URL in this section of your page. Otherwise, it gets buried in the full 'About' description that's not visible unless a person clicks on the 'About' link on your page. Make it easy for people to learn more about your brand by making sure your URL is visible in the top-level 'About' section.

The above sections constitute your landing page, which essentially should tell the viewer everything they need to know very quickly (masses of text are a turn-off to most Facebook users). Think about what a visitor will want to know when he or she visits – 'what is this site about?' and 'where do I click?'. You need to create a great-looking and interesting landing page to encourage visitors to explore and ultimately 'like' your page.

To add more interest to your landing page, install free apps and add content such as events and videos to provide more diverse experiences to your audience. Make sure the most interesting ones are front and centre. These are the ones that will be automatically visible in the app thumbnails section of your Facebook page beneath your cover photo. Your Photos tab is cemented in the first position, but the others can be moved. On all but the Likes tab, you can also upload a custom image, which can further cement your branding.

Once your page is set up, ask all of your Facebook friends to like it. This is a great way to get the ball rolling and start building a following.

## NEXT STEPS

After the initial setup (which could take several hours), the next step is creating interesting, meaningful, useful or entertaining content that your target audience wants to read and see. This includes uploading compelling posts and photos of your crafts. Remember a Facebook page without content is one that no one will like. Keep your copy tight and try to limit your post to ninety characters, or at least make sure any links appear in the first ninety characters. To increase engagement, pose your post as a question. It is best practice to devote ten minutes a day to your Facebook page to reap the most rewards.

Why ten minutes? There are numerous reasons why, but most important, Facebook can help strengthen your relationship with your customers. The smaller your business, the more important these connections can be to help keep your craft business thriving. Highlighting the human factor of your company is what creates strong relationships between you and your customers, and as I said previously, the story behind your crafts is very important.

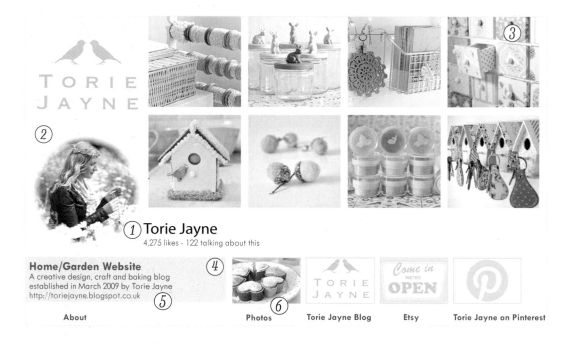

**1.** Use your craft brand name as your username for consistency. Establish this as soon as possible in order to claim the name you wish to use.

**2.** This is the smaller image that appears on your Facebook page and as your Facebook avatar. See pages 60–61 for advice on picking and designing an avatar.

**3.** Add Timeline cover photos to showcase your crafts and represent your brand.

**4.** This is the 'About' section where you can describe your craft business in a few sentences. The text should include plenty of keywords in order to ensure these come up in people's searches.

**5.** Include your website URL in the 'About' section. Place it near the top so it is immediately visible to anyone browsing your page.

**6.** These sections together constitute your landing page, and rely on snappy text and attractive images to let viewers know exactly what they can expect.

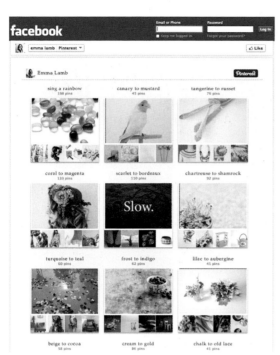

- Don't have time to publish a lot of content on your Facebook page? No problem. You can automate some publishing by feeding your blog posts and Twitter updates to your page. But don't rely solely on auto posting; you should make a concerted effort to post unique content to Facebook.

- Use Facebook social plug-ins to enable people to like your page directly from your website and blog, or to like your website or blog content and share it on their own Facebook profiles with a single click.

- Provide as many details as possible in the full 'About' description. Fill in as much basic information as you can to tell your entire story and fully explain what your craft business does.

- Interact with customers straight from your smartphone.

- Don't just try to sell, sell, sell. On Facebook, as with all social media, you won't last long if you only write about what you are selling every day. Be more creative and build up relationships by letting your potential customers know more about you personally, by talking about your creative process or sharing your inspiration.

- Give fans something they can't get anywhere else.

## TERMINOLOGY

### LIKE
A method of endorsing another page in order to be kept up-to-date with its activity.

### NOTIFICATION
An alert which informs you of activity on your page, such as a comment or question.

### STATUS
A tool for keeping visitors informed of everything you are currently doing.

# PINTEREST

*Pinterest*

Pinterest is a virtual pinboard, a photo-sharing social media site for collecting, organising and sharing the different things you find and love on the web. While other social networks, like Facebook and Twitter, focus on personal sharing and status updates, Pinterest is driven entirely by visuals. You can't share something on Pinterest unless an image or video is involved.

Founded in 2010, Pinterest was the first social media site to hit 10 million users in less than two years. It is hailed as one of the top ten social networks in terms of active population. How do you as a crafter make the most of Pinterest?

- Remember people use Pinterest for visual inspiration, for wish lists, and for organising and sharing ideas that are best expressed with pictures. Ideally you want people to pin and repin your crafts and hopefully add your crafts to their wish lists. It is ultimately another way to get more exposure.

- When creating a Pinterest account, you can choose to connect your Twitter and Facebook accounts along with your website. Use Pinterest's social plugins to enable people to follow your page directly from your website or blog. Create pins whenever you do a good blog post, using the best images with a simple description. That way, the source site will encourage others to look at your blog and join you on other social media platforms. Also, share your pins on Twitter and Facebook to encourage fans of your other social media sites to join you on Pinterest.

- Devote ten minutes a day to Pinterest. In order to have a Pinterest account that is useful and helps promote your brand and crafts, you have to incorporate it into your regular social media practice. It's better to pin a few things every day than to flood your followers' feed once a month. If people see your pins coming up again and again, they will follow you.

- Use keywords in your description box and help your would-be followers discover your content by including relevant and pleasing descriptions. Keep your images high-quality and interesting.

- Keep it varied, and don't just pin your finished products. If you fill your boards with numerous images of the same craft, people could easily get annoyed and turned off from even visiting. Share your visual inspiration and colour palettes for upcoming craft collections you are working on. It can be a great way to get a buzz about your new collection and help your customers understand the theory behind your brand.

- Just because you sell a particular craft does not mean that you should pin only the items related to that craft. As explained earlier in branding, you are the brand, so feel free to pin any of the things you love. This is a great way of sharing you and your style, which, after all, is your brand.

## TIPS

- Remember to be good about attribution. Take the time to check that the images you are pinning link to the correct source. People use Pinterest to find cool things. If you find something cool, tell people where you found it. After all, if someone pins one of your crafts, you want everyone to be able to know it is yours and where they can purchase it. If you upload a pin without attribution, that's rude (and could be illegal).

- As well as self-promotion and brand-building, Pinterest can be a great tool to keep all kinds of information you find on the Internet organised and accessible. So if you find a great tutorial on blogging or account keeping, pin it to a secret board that you can use and keep coming back to without ruining the look of your carefully curated, stylish brand boards.

## TERMINOLOGY

### PIN

A pin is an image or video you share on Pinterest. You can add a pin from a website using the 'Pin It bookmarklet' or upload an image right from your computer. Any pin on Pinterest can be repinned, and all pins link back to their source.

### PIN IT BOOKMARKLET

This is a bookmarking tool that installs on your web browser toolbar that lets you easily pin any image or video you find when browsing the Internet.

### REPIN

When you share someone else's pin on Pinterest, it's called a repin.

### BOARD

A board is where you organise your pins by topic, style or colour. You could pin ideas for your living room, wedding, or create an inspiration board – whatever interests you. Boards can be public or secret, and you can invite other people to pin on your boards.

### FOLLOW

When you follow someone, their pins appear in your Pinterest home feed. You can follow all of someone's boards or just the ones you like.

# TWITTER

Twitter is a social networking site and real-time communication and microblogging service that enables its users to send and read small bursts of text-based messages of up to 140 characters known as 'tweets'. You can see photos, videos and conversations directly in tweets to get the whole story at a glance, and all in one place. Twitter was launched in 2006 in San Francisco and is used by millions of people and organisations in nearly every country in the world.

With over 400 million tweets a day and 200 million active users, Twitter can be a powerful tool for your craft brand. People tune into Twitter to bring them closer to the things they care about.

First, pick a username for your Twitter 'handle'. Make it short and sweet and preferably your brand name. Next, create your bio, with a little bit of information about you, your crafts and your interests, to help people get to know more about you and decide whether they'd like to follow you. You can also include your location, website link and an avatar image (page 60). Try to add some of your brand styling to your page with a neat background image and cover photo, and incorporate your brand colours.

Get tweeting! You can post tweets of up to 140 characters. These tweets can also have media embedded such as photos, videos or snippets from articles, which will make your tweets more engaging for your followers (research shows that photographs generally get twice the attention compared to regular text posts).

## TIPS

- Use Twitter to let your followers know when you have new products for sale. Make sure you embed a photo of your new craft.

- Automate posts.

- Don't over-tweet. You don't want to fill your followers' feed with tweets just from you or they may be turned off and stop following you.

- Favourite related tweets to your crafts, style and brand. To help the process, you should search for keywords that are relevant to your interests.

- Create a user widget for your website by going to the Gear Icon > Settings > Widgets > Create New. The widget will display your tweets, and you can customise how it looks.

*'I blog several times a week and have built up a decent following. I don't always blog about my products, which helps keep my readers' attention. I post peeks into my sketchbook, DIY projects, recipes, my photography, and more. When I create new designs, I announce them on my blog, and I also post new products on Twitter, Facebook and Pinterest.'*
Amanda Wright, Wit & Whistle

## TERMINOLOGY

### A TWEET
A standard message on Twitter containing 140 characters or less.

### RETWEET
A tweet that has been shared or reposted by another user to his/her followers.

### HASHTAG
In Twitter, the # symbol is used to tag keywords or topics in a tweet to make it easily identifiable for search purposes.

### MENTION
Tweets can include replies and mentions of other users by preceding their usernames with the @ sign.

### HANDLE
Your username and accompanying URL at http://twitter.com/handle.

### FEED
The stream of tweets on your Twitter homepage comprised of all the accounts you follow.

### LISTS
Twitter provides a mechanism to list the users you follow into groups or curated lists.

### DIRECT MESSAGE
Also called a DM, this represents Twitter's direct messaging system for private communication among users.

# INSTAGRAM

Instagram

Like Twitter and Facebook, Instagram is a great promotional tool.

Instagram is an online photo- and video-sharing and social networking service that enables its users to save and share photos and videos. Photos, which are confined to square shapes, have different filters you can use to make them more interesting. You can take pictures within the app or use photos that already exist in your camera. You can give your photo a title, which is helpful and fun, and add descriptive hashtags. Photos can be shared instantly, not only on Instagram, but also on Facebook, Twitter, Flickr and Tumblr.

On Instagram you 'follow' people. Search for your favourite brands, crafters and creatives and follow them. You can see which of your Twitter and Facebook friends are using Instagram so you can easily start following them. Comment on and 'like' photos you admire and find visually appealing. The more photos you 'like', the more your name/brand will pop up on Instagram.

Instagram is purely visual, which is perfect for crafters. To get started, go to the App Store, download, set up your account, choose a username and upload a profile picture. It is that easy!

## TIPS

- Adding tags to your photos is a great way to find new followers and share your photos with more people. Make it easy for other like-minded Instagrammers to find you by making sure your tags describe your photos. Be specific with your hashtags so the photo will be added to the highly targeted tag page. Pay attention to the other hashtags used on photos that use the same tag as yours. You may discover a popular hashtag you hadn't thought of on your own.

- Brighten up your underexposed photos with a single tap! When the lighting isn't great, use the Lux button to transform your picture into a lovely detailed shot.

- As well as showing your products, you should also appeal to your audience. Give fans something they can't get anywhere else, like shots of your work in progress and photos of your craft inspiration, such as colours, objects and shapes you like.

- Emulate your style and brand through your photo stream.

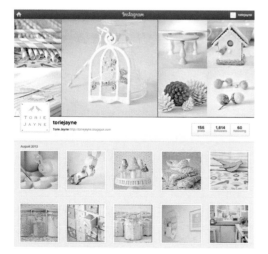

# FLICKR

Flickr (pronounced 'flicker') is an image- and video-hosting website, web services suite and online community that was created by Ludicorp in 2004 and acquired by Yahoo! in 2005. In addition to being a popular website for users to share and embed personal photographs, the service is widely used by bloggers to host images that they embed in blogs and social media.

Flickr is one of the best ways to store, sort, search and share your photos online. It differs from Instagram because you are able to upload photos of any size and resolution and easily organise them into sets. You can also add your photos to groups, as well as 'like' and comment on other photos.

But Flickr is more than just a simple photo storage site; it is actually a powerful tool for craft shops to reach customers and to promote products. When your photos of your crafts start collecting more 'likes' and are more frequent in search queries, your craft brand will naturally get more exposure. You can also make 'contacts' (similar to 'friends' or 'followers' on other sites). Your contacts will see your photos on their Flickr homepage and of course they can click on you any time to check out your photos. Many people use Flickr to offer their work under the Creative Commons license which reduces the amount of restrictions imposed by regular copyright legislation.

## TIPS

- Send your photos to the groups that you join to get more exposure. You can find groups at www.flickr.com/groups/. Make sure you read the rules on each group's page.

- Use your brand name as a tag on all your craft photos.

# BLOGGING

You need a blog, even if you have an Etsy shop. A blog helps you build a relationship with your potential customers. People want to do business with people they like, and having a blog is a great way to form that relationship.

A blog is a particular type of website that consists of articles (more commonly referred to as posts), usually date stamped and organised in reverse chronology so that the reader always sees the most recent post first. It fundamentally works on the basis that you: 1) log onto the admin pages of your blog; 2) write your post and upload images and photos, etc.; 3) publish the post. Instantly your words, images and photographs appear on your blog, automatically formatted and added to precious posts in the layout and style that you have set up.

There are two main platforms for blogging: Blogger, a free service from Google, or WordPress. For further information see online resources (page 130).

Your blog is your own voice, and it is fair to say that not everyone will agree with everything you say all of the time. Handling rude or critical comments can be one of the hardest things about blogging, especially if it seems or is taken personally. It is advisable to adjust your comments settings to moderate comments before they go live. If someone leaves a negative comment, it is up to you if you publish it. If you feel it is legitimate criticism, you can address it in a polite and professional manner. Dealing with difficult comments in the correct way can earn you a huge amount of respect from sympathetic onlookers.

## TIPS

- Try to post at least once a week. When you start posting more frequently, subscriptions, followers, page views and comments all tend to improve.

- Show off your crafts.

- Write inspiring blog post titles.

- Never commit to anything you can't follow through with. Having a sewing Sunday, for instance, is no good if you aren't going to do it for more than a month, because your readers will expect it regularly. When you fail to deliver, you could lose followers. Avoid committing to any particular day or promising weekly commitments you can't keep.

- Automatic music on a blog is generally a big no-no. Just because you share a passion for pastels with your followers doesn't mean they share your love for Madonna!

- Want blog comments? You will get them if you serve as a commenter too.

- Ask friends with blogs for blog post swaps so you both can share your work.

## MEET THE CRAFTERS
## CITY CHIC COUNTRY MOUSE

Jamie Halleckson and Carmen Marti from City Chic Country Mouse, began a venture combining mum's (Country Mouse) sewing talent with daughter's (City Chic) sense of style. They love to create items that inspire people in their homes by making boring household chores more enjoyable.

*'There are so many wonderful resources online. We love to read blogs and just click from one site to another. We probably sometimes spend too much time online!'*

From the sewing studio to the utility room and kitchen, they enjoy bringing style to these everyday household tasks. It all started with the handing down of a thirty-year-old Singer sewing machine (from Country Mouse to City Chic) and both falling in love with some fabric at a local fabric store. Who knew it would blossom into an unbelievably enjoyable joint venture?

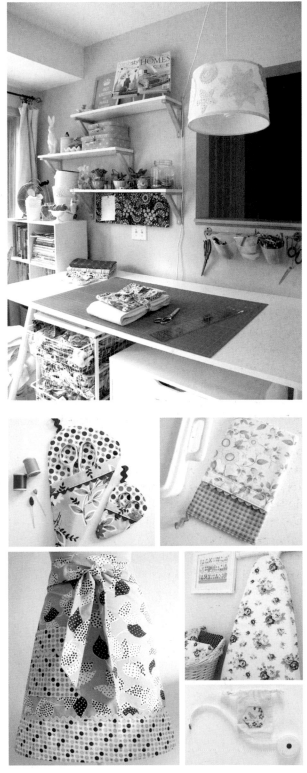

# GETTING NOTICED

Stay active about marketing your business. If you don't market it, no one else will.

Publicity in a pretty broad term basically means getting featured in the media. This could be in a traditional media outlet, such as a newspaper, or it could mean being featured in a blog post, which is now considered new media. Contact bloggers whose design aesthetic fits in with yours.

First impressions count for everything when contacting a blogger, so before pitching your idea or asking them to feature you, make sure your photography is the best. Most bloggers hold high standards for photos as the pictures and graphics on a blog tell a story and help them maintain a theme. Your photography should fit in with the overall style and

aesthetic of their site. Next you must do your research before talking to any blogger, myself included. Two of the worst things you can do are: 1) write an email that seems like you have never visited or read the blog; and 2) send a story idea that has already been covered or has nothing to do with the blog. Some of the best pitches I have received reference a recent post and make it obvious they understand my design aesthetic by mentioning my featured colours and style.

So you have picked a blog, done your research, and your photos are immaculate. Now it is time to write the perfect pitch. Start with a great subject line that will capture the blogger's attention. Believe me, bloggers get hundreds of email requests a week and yours needs to stand out. Make sure you are personable, polite, and address the blogger by name. (Spell their name correctly. I can't tell you the number of times I receive emails that spell my name incorrectly, which does not set a good impression.) Do not send out mass emails. Just email one blogger at a time and do not pitch by Facebook or Twitter. Make your pitch short, sharp and punchy, and engage with the blogger in one or two paragraphs.

Include links to your shop, blog or website. Include two to three low-res images and always proofread and spell-check your message before sending. It is fine to send a follow-up email to touch base again if you have not received a reply after a week. Finally, last but not least, if you are featured on a blog, be sure to send a follow-up thank you email.

## IDEAS FOR PUBLICITY

Remember, enthusiasm is infectious. Let all your colleagues know about your crafts. Tell all your friends, your family, people you meet at parties or at the beauty salon.

Do you have an email signature? An email signature is a collection of words, images, links, or all three that you choose to appear in your outgoing emails. Think of all the emails you send out. Each of those emails could be telling all the recipients about your company, Facebook Page, Twitter, and all your other social media. It's free advertising with no added effort.

Start a newsletter to stay in contact with your customers and potential customers. MailChimp is a free option, or if you are selling through Etsy, you could try AWeber. Develop and maintain a mailing list by capturing details at events and taking them from your customers. Use it to make regular contact. Then, host competitions on your social websites in which you give away some of your crafts.

Get used to writing short press releases on significant developments in your business. Have you won an award or prize? Have you appeared in a magazine article? Send a short and snappy press release with a high-resolution photograph to your local media. They love a good local story.

### TIPS

- Donate one of your crafts to a local charity auction.

- Offer friends and family an incentive for marketing your crafts.

- Make sure you are listed in any relevant craft directories.

- Enter and try to win relevant craft design contests.

- Consider teaching your crafts to others at centres, craft stores and schools. You will become known as an expert in your craft.

- Provide excellent customer service. Be professional at all times. Keep to your agreements and deadlines and communicate clearly and regularly with all your customers.

- Build a group of followers and elicit their responses.

- Curate content and join the conversation.

- Experiment with keyword research.

- Build profiles on other sites.

- Update by assessing and reassessing.

Write guest posts. This is a simple but effective way to start building some buzz for your brand. Work with other bloggers by sending them products to review or give away. Be strategic and careful that you don't give away too much. When you are just starting to market your craft, remember that everyone starts out small. Yes, even Martha Stewart started out in her basement.

If you sell a craft that's wearable, such as jewellery, make sure you have a piece on when you go out. Show off your work! This shows pride in your work and illustrates how well your pieces can be worn.

# WORDS
# OF WISDOM

'Starting crafting has been a wonderful way of "starting" a new career in illustration for me. It really helped me create my world and style, and made me see my job in a different light. I work very differently now than before crafting. It's a lot more personal.'
Anne Cresci, Matilou (page 107)

'Stay true to your own ideas and skills and don't be too inspired by the industry you work in. It helps to ensure, in a certain way, that you stand out. Being creative means you are constantly spinning in your own whirlpool of ideas. I spend a lot of time on my own as a lot of makers do, and as much as I love my studio and what I do, you can go a little stir crazy. Invest a small proportion of time in making arrangements to see/meet people/clients/friends outside of your working environment.'
Vicky Trainor (page 97)

'It is certainly true that you must love what you do if you want to be successful. Building a business is not a nine-to-five job.'
City Chic Country Mouse (page 125)

'You need a great deal of support around you when you start a craft business. If you are sharing your life with someone, you need them on your side because, like with any business, you inevitably have to make some sacrifices that will affect you both. I would never have gotten this far with Three Red Apples if it wasn't for my other half helping me ride the highs and lows.'
Annabelle Ozanne, Three Red Apples
(page 49)

'Time is in short supply. There is more inspiration than time to act on it.'
Helena Schaeder Söderberg,
Craft & Creativity (page 22)

'It's a process. If I had waited to open my shop until I was awesome at everything, I'd never have started my business at all. You don't need to have everything figured out before you begin. As long as you have a general idea of where you're headed, you'll work things out and find your niche along the way. The important thing is to take that first step and get going.'
Amanda Wright, Wit & Whistle (page 58)

'I think the biggest lesson is to somehow figure out your goal. I say this as someone who doesn't often write my goals on paper but instead has this vision in my mind of what I want. Asking yourself a few questions might help you arrive at a plan; questions such as, am I selling to make a few extra pounds, to simply fund my crafting pastime, to earn a living, etc.? Knowing the answers to these questions will help you figure out what you need to do to make the craft business work for you personally as you go forward. I learned that I enjoyed the writing about as much as the making and soon shifted from seller to writer to author.'
Elyse Major, Tinkered Treasures (page 42)

'Maintain a positive frame of mind and outlook at all times. Putting your work and yourself out there invites lots of positive and rewarding feedback but will also attract unreasonable negativity. This is an unavoidable fact and one that no one can truly prepare themselves for. My advice is to surround yourself with positive friends and family (both online and offline). Educate yourself about how you can take proactive steps to resolve an ugly situation and carry them out if you need to; if there is a persistent cause of unhappiness do not be afraid to remove it from your situation (social media platforms have un-friend options for just this reason!).'
Emma Lamb (page 14)

'You need to do something you enjoy when you start a business. Business can be tough, you work really hard, and in the beginning it seems you are doing so much and making little money. You have to love what you do to be able to stick it out until you grow. That is the joy of owning a business rather than working for someone. You have the freedom to do something you enjoy.'
Tabitha Emma (page 113)

# ONLINE RESOURCES

## USEFUL WEBSITES

Here are some useful resources that will help you research and understand the topics covered. At the time of writing this book I have tried to be as accurate as possible. However, websites do come and go and any specific address may change from what is written here. Your best bet is to try searching for the site; if you get nothing, it is probably safe to assume that the site is now closed.

For an up-to-date resources list, please visit my website, toriejayne.com, where I will endeavour to keep the list current. I will also inform you of any new, exciting websites and social networks that I feel would aid you in showing and selling your crafts.

## CRAFT SHOPS
### UK
Panduro Hobby:
    www.pandurohobby.co.uk

Hobbycraft:
    www.hobbycraft.co.uk

Fred Aldous:
    www.fredaldous.co.uk

Superlovely (for washi tape)
    www.superlovely.com

Amazon: www.amazon.co.uk

eBay: www.ebay.co.uk

Liberty's Haberdashery:
    www.liberty.co.uk

Cloth House, Soho London:
    www.clothhouse.com

VV Rouleaux (for ribbons):
    www.vvrouleaux.com

### USA
Jo-Ann Stores:
    www.joann.com

Michaels:
    www.michaels.com

Paper Source:
    www.paper-source.com

## SCANDINAVIA
Panduro Hobby:
    www.pandurohobby.com

## ONLINE MARKETPLACES
Etsy: www.etsy.com

Folksy: www.folksy.com

Big Cartel: www.bigcartel.com

Art Fire: www.artfire.com

DaWanda: en.dawanda.com

Made It: www.madeit.com.au

## BLOG HOSTING OPTIONS
Blogger: www.blogger.com

WordPress: www.wordpress.com

Typepad: www.typepad.com

BlogPress: www.theblogpress.com

## CRAFT SHOWS
### UK
Twisted Thread:
    www.twistedthread.com

ICHF:
    www.ichfevents.co.uk

## USA
Renegade Craft Fairs:
    www.renegadecraft.com

American Craft Council Show:
    www.craftcouncil.org

## FREE PHOTO EDITORS
Picasa: www.picasa.google.com
    Free photo editing software
    from Google

Aviary: www.aviary.com
    Web-based photo editing
    with lots of fun tools

Photoshop Express Editor:
    www.photoshop.com/tools
    Resize and add text to
    your images

PicMonkey: www.picmonkey.com
    Resize and add text to your
    images, with an array of
    fun tools

## DOMAIN NAMES
www.godaddy.com

www.register.com

www.ukwebsolutions.co.uk

www.namesecure.com

## COMPANY NAME REGISTERS AND TRADEMARKS

www.secstates.com

www.ipo.gov.uk

www.companieshouse.gov.uk

www.copyright.gov

## BUSINESS HELP AND MARKETING

Business Link:
www.businesslink.gov.uk

SBDC (Small Business
Development Centre):
www.sba.gov

Creative business cards:
www.moo.com

MailChimp: www.mailchimp.com

Constant Contact: www.
constantcontact.com

SurveyMonkey: www.
surveymonkey.com

Wufoo: www.wufoo.com

## POSTAGE AND SHIPPING

US Postage:
www.usps.com

UPS (United Parcel Service):
www.ups.com

FedEx: www.fedex.com

Canadian postal tools:
www.canadapost.ca/
cpo/mc/business/tools/
electronicshippingtool.jsf

Australian Post Postage Calculator:
http://auspost.com.au/apps/
postage-calculator.html

UK Royal Mail Price Finder:
http://www.royalmail.com/
price-finder

DPD Shipping Calculator:
http://www.dpd.com/nl_en/
home/shipping/shipping_
international2/delivery_time_
calculator

# WHAT NEXT?

You've perfected your crafts, created your business and developed an effective marketing strategy – now what? The decisions you make on a daily basis will affect the future of your business, so it's worth always keeping one eye on the horizon and staying focused on your goals. Before you do this, though, you need to work out what those goals are. Consider branching out into alternative fields, or teaching your skills to others. Host events in order to market your business, and always keep on top of the latest trends and current events in the crafting world. Here is some helpful advice on things you should consider as you plan your next steps into the wonderful world of crafting and beyond. Best of luck, and enjoy the journey!

## EXPLORING FURTHER AFIELD

We are all multitalented. Crafting involves a wide range of skills that transfer easily between tasks. If you can work with detail or mould polymer clay, then why not try patisserie and sugarcraft? If your colour palettes excite customers and you have a passion for homewares, have you considered interior design? Building a strong brand means that there's almost no limit to what you can create. Stay true to your design philosophy and widen your horizons to attract more customers, investments and opportunities. You can open your craft business up to new platforms, from blogging communities and professional directories to different trade shows and shops.

As well as handcrafted products, you could think about offering services at an hourly or daily rate. Play to your strengths – it doesn't cost anything to highlight your expertise on a website, blog or newsletter, and you might be able to turn that eye for vintage-inspired design into a larger, more profitable project. You never know who might be looking for an inspiring wedding planner or a consultant on boutique hotel décor.

## TEACHING YOUR CRAFT

Teaching craft is all about sharing your passion for creating with others. The next natural step for you as a successful crafter might be to share your expertise with others. Teaching craft classes is not only fun, rewarding and social but can also be an additional means of making a little extra money. You don't have to share everything – keeping some essential creative secrets to yourself will protect your unique brand. Teaching craft workshops can help to promote your brand by demonstrating the appeal of handmade objects to people who are new to crafting.

There are many options open to you on how to go about teaching your craft. You don't have to be a natural public speaker or have all the time in the world. Options include lunchtime classes at work, online tutorials that you can blog or post on social media, evening classes at home or in a rented venue, one-off workshops and school groups.

- Don't feel that you have to go it alone — reach out to fellow crafters and suggest holding joint events that combine homemade craft and cookery.

- It is a good idea to run free practise classes if you decide to charge. Invite your friends and family and hand out feedback forms each time you teach.

- Research the legalities, for example first-aid training and business insurance.

## HOSTING EVENTS

As a professional crafter you can use your craft to host fun events that benefit local communities. Use your imagination with invites and utilise all your social media channels to invite all your dedicated followers. Events might include charity fundraisers, sales in your home, craft fairs, competitions and local school workshops.

Keep an eye on the calendar too as seasonal celebrations create a demand for craft-related events, so take advantage of this, get clued up on what's happening around you and let your business reap the benefits.

## CONTINUING TO RESEARCH

You know how vital market research is to setting up your business, but you might not have thought about its importance in making consistent profits long-term. Seasons and trends change – you need to make sure that your brand stays fresh, exciting, innovative and market friendly.

This may be as simple as keeping an eye on the price of comparable products. You don't want to be far above or below that mark, and they will fluctuate. Also, new mass-produced devices such as mobile phones and tablets may become popular and give you inspiration. You don't need to change your design aesthetic to coincide with colour trends, just adapt to the seasons. Most importantly, however, you need to research the market on a regular basis to make sure that your work is not being copied without accreditation. Keep up to date and take legal advice if necessary.

## RELOCATING YOUR BUSINESS

So your craft room is a beautiful, inspiring space that reflects your brand and your personality. Now what do you do when every spare square-metre is packed with innovative storage solutions and there still isn't enough room? Well, one of the hallmarks of your success might be the need to relocate. Whether it's because your crafts are getting bigger – maybe you're exploring the world of customised furniture – or because you need to accommodate an employee or two, relocating can be an extremely rewarding experience that really helps to build your business. Here are a few useful tips to make the process as stress-free as possible.

First, think about relocating as an opportunity rather than a hassle. You can redesign a whole new space, whether it's a studio or workshop. Then, make sure you tell customers you are moving. Use your social networking platforms, your email signature, your newsletter mailing list, and generate some buzz about your fresh start. If possible, try to move over a weekend or holiday to avoid disruption to shipping. Plan carefully – does your new space need to dry out before pretty papers can be left there? Enlist the help of friends to relocate your stock and materials, label all boxes, and set up your new Internet connection as soon as possible.

## HIRING HELP

If your craft room has a 'Help Wanted' sign, then you're definitely on the road to success. Whether you need a few extra pairs of hands for assembling your products, or just want a little administrative support, being the boss entitles you to hire some help.

Your friends will want to help you out – resist the temptation. It might seem like a good idea to hire people you know, but the employer–employee relationship means you need to tell people what to do, which can cause friction, especially where money is concerned. Consider taking someone on as work experience, and focus on hiring skilled people with the appropriate skills and qualifications.

Ask for a cover letter and CV, and check out applicants' social networking sites. Ask new employees to sign a non-disclosure agreement protecting your intellectual property. Otherwise, make sure you provide a safe workplace and have the correct insurance coverage, and do the research and get professional advice on the minefields that can be payroll and taxes.

## WORK–LIFE BALANCE

Your craft represents so much of your personality that sometimes it's difficult to put down the scissors, needles, and brushes and take a step back. Everyone knows your business is important to you, but it's also important to relax, unwind, and take care of yourself too. A healthy and happy crafter is a successful one, so try to maintain your work–life balance.

It sounds simple, but make time for your friends and family. Laughing and having fun with those you love fuels your creative streak, and it feels pretty good too. Make sure you're eating properly. TV dinners and takeaways are OK when you're trying to meet a deadline, but your health and work will suffer if you do this too often. Likewise, exercise is crucial for crafters. You tend to spend hour after hour in unnatural, hunched-over positions, and repetitive strain injuries are common. Stand up, stretch your neck and shoulders, and go for a short walk. Then take a nap – you probably need it!

# SOCIAL MEDIA SUMMARY

## WWW.TWITTER.COM

Twitter is an online social networking site and microblogging service that enables its users to send and read text-based messages of up to 140 characters, which are known as 'tweets'.

## WWW.FACEBOOK.COM

Facebook users can create pages allowing fans of an individual, organisation, product, service or concept to like or subscribe to the page posts and updates. Pages look and behave much like a user's personal private profile, but they are also integrated with Facebook's advertising system, allowing owners to easily advertise to Facebook's users. Owners (admins) can send updates to their fans, and they also have access to insights and analytics of their fan base. While an individual with a personal profile can acquire up to 5,000 friends, a Facebook page can have an unlimited number of 'likes' and subscribers. Pages can also be customised by adding new third-party apps, presented in a form of tab icons on a page.

## WWW.INSTAGRAM.COM

Instagram is an online photo-sharing and social networking service that enables its users to take pictures, apply digital filters to them, and share them on a variety of social networking services, such as Facebook or Twitter. A distinctive feature is that it confines photos to a square shape.

## WWW.PINTEREST.COM

Pinterest is a pinboard-style photo-sharing website that allows users to create and manage theme-based image collections such as events, interests and hobbies. Users can browse other pinboards for images, repin images to their own pinboards, or 'like' photos.

## WWW.FLICKR.COM

Flickr (stylised as flickr and pronounced 'flicker') is an image- and video-hosting website, web services suite and online community that was created by Ludicorp in 2004 and acquired by Yahoo! in 2005. In addition to being a popular website for users to share and embed personal photographs, the service is widely used by bloggers to host images that they embed in blogs and social media.

## WWW.LINKEDIN.COM

LinkedIn is a social networking website for people in professional occupations. Launched in May 2003, it is mainly used for professional networking. As of January 2013, LinkedIn reports more than 200 million acquired users in more than 200 countries and territories.

## WWW.GOOGLE.CO.UK/ANALYTICS

Google Analytics is a free web-based tool, which you can use to find out a huge amount of information that can be beneficial to you in attracting more of the traffic you are looking for and help you turn more visitors into customers.

# CRAFTERS

## ANNE CRESCI, *FRANCE*
### BRAND: MATILOU

**Blog:** http://annecresci.blogspot.co.uk
**Etsy:** http://www.etsy.com/uk/shop/matilou
**Facebook Page:** https://www.facebook.com/pages/
Matilou/74363959220
**Twitter:** https://twitter.com/matilou
**Flickr:** http://www.flickr.com/photos/23136898@N08

## NELLIANNA VAN DEN BAARD, KENNETH VEENENBOS, FLEUR VAN DUSSELDORP, *NETHERLANDS*
### BRAND: STUDIO SNOWPUPPE

**Website:** http://www.studiosnowpuppe.nl
**Facebook Page:** https://www.facebook.com/pages/
Studio-Snowpuppe/203615149666763?sk=wall
**Twitter:** https://twitter.com/snowpuppe
**Instagram:** http://instagram.com/snowpuppe
**Flickr:** http://www.flickr.com/photos/
studiosnowpuppe
**YouTube:** http://www.youtube.com/user/
snowpuppe#p/u/3/3N10KT1O-7g

## TABITHA EMMA, *AUSTRALIA*
### BRAND: TABITHA EMMA

**Website:** http://tabithaemma.com
**Blog:** http://tabithaemma.com/blog
**Etsy:** http://www.etsy.com/shop/tabithaemma
**Facebook Page:** https://www.facebook.com/pages/
Tabitha-Emma/231351125905
**Twitter:** https://twitter.com/tabithaemma
**Pinterest:** http://pinterest.com/tabithaemma
**Dribbble:** http://dribbble.com/tabithaemma
**Instagram:** http://instagram.com/tabithaemma

## JAMIE HALLECKSON & CARMEN MARTI, *USA*
### BRAND: CITY CHIC COUNTRY MOUSE

**Website:** www.CityChicCountryMouse.com

**Blog:** http://citychiccountrymouse.blogspot.co.uk
**Etsy:** www.etsy.com/shop/citychiccountrymouse
**Facebook Page:** www.facebook/
CityChicCountryMouse
**Twitter:** twitter.com/CityChicJamie
**Pinterest:** http://pinterest.com/jamieh
**Instagram:** lucyjunesmama

## TORIE JAYNE, *UK*
### BRAND: TORIE JAYNE

**Website:** http://toriejayne.com
**Etsy:** http://www.etsy.com/shop/TorieJayne
**Blog:** http://toriejayne.blogspot.co.uk
**Facebook Page:** https://www.facebook.com/
TorieJayneBlog
**Twitter:** https://twitter.com/Toriejayne
**Flickr:** http://www.flickr.com/photos/toriejayne
**Pinterest:** http://pinterest.com/toriejayne
**Instagram:** http://instagram.com/toriejayne

## EMMA LAMB, *UK*
### BRAND: EMMA LAMB

**Blog** http://emmallamb.blogspot.co.uk
**Etsy:** https://www.etsy.com/shop/emmalamb
**Folksy:** http://folksy.com/shops/emmalamb
**Ravelry:** http://www.ravelry.com/designers/
emma-lamb
**Shop:** http://emmallamb.blogspot.co.uk/p/patterns.
html
**Facebook Page:** https://www.facebook.com/
emmalamb.uk
**Pinterest:** http://pinterest.com/emmalamb/pins
**Flickr:** http://www.flickr.com/photos/emmalamb
**Bloglovin':** http://www.bloglovin.com/emmallamb

## ELYSE MAJOR, *USA*
### BRAND: TINKERED TREASURES

**Website:** tinkeredtreasures.com
**Blog:** tinkeredtreasures.blogspot.co.uk
**Etsy:** http://www.etsy.com/shop/tinkeredtreasures
**Facebook Page:** www.facebook.com/
ElyseMajorTinkeredTreasures
**Twitter:** twitter.com/tinkeredtreasrs
**Pinterest:** pinterest.com/tinkeredtreasrs

**Flickr:** http://www.flickr.com/photos/elysemajor
**Bloglovin':** http://www.bloglovin.com/en/blog/1582149
**LinkedIn:** www.linkedin.com/in/elysemajor
**Goodreads:** http://www.goodreads.com/author/show/6902169.Elyse_Major

## ANNABELLE OZANNE, *UK*
## BRAND: THREE RED APPLES

**Website:** www.threeredapples.com
**Blog:** http://www.threeredapples.blogspot.co.uk
**Etsy:** http://www.etsy.com/shop/threeredapples
**Facebook Page:** www.facebook.com/threeredapples
**Twitter:** twitter.com/threeredapples
**Flickr:** www.flickr.com/photos/threeredapples
**Bloglovin':** http://www.bloglovin.com/blog/2168859/three-red-apples

## HELENA SCHAEDER SÖDERBERG, *SWEDEN*
## BRAND: CRAFT & CREATIVITY

**Website:** http://www.makeandcreate.se
**Blog:** http://craftandcreativity.com/blog
**Facebook Page:** https://www.facebook.com/pages/Craft-Creativity/255215084531333
**Pinterest:** http://pinterest.com/craftcreativity
**Instagram:** http://instagram.com/craft_and_creativity
**Flickr:** http://www.flickr.com/photos/craftcreativity
**Tumblr:** http://craftandcreativity.tumblr.com
**Bloglovin':** http://www.bloglovin.com/en/blog/3044314

## TAMAR SCHECHNER, *USA*
## BRAND: NEST PRETTY THINGS

**Website:** http://nestprettythings.com
**Blog:** http://nestprettythings.com/journal
**Etsy:** http://www.etsy.com/shop/NestPrettyThingsShop?ref=si_shop
http://www.etsy.com/shop/nestprettythingskids
http://www.etsy.com/shop/nestprettybrides
**Facebook Page:** https://www.facebook.com/nestprettythings
**Flickr:** http://www.flickr.com/photos/12558159@N08
**Tumblr:** http://nestprettythings.tumblr.com

## WHITNEY SMITH, *USA*
## BRAND: WHITNEY SMITH

**Website:** www.whitneysmithpottery.com
**Blog:** http://whitneys-pottery.blogspot.co.uk
**Shop:** www.whitneysmithpottery.com/#!shop
**Etsy:** www.etsy.com/shop/whitneysmith
**Facebook Page:** www.facebook.com/WhitneySmithPottery
**Twitter:** https://twitter.com/whitneyspottery
**Flickr:** www.flickr.com/photos/poppygirl/6842019081

## MEL STRINGER, *AUSTRALIA*
## BRAND: GIRLIE PAINS

**Website:** http://melstringer.storenvy.com
**Blog:** http://melstringer.blogspot.co.uk
**Shop:** http://melstringer.storenvy.com
**Etsy:** http://www.etsy.com/shop/girliepains
**Facebook Page:** https://www.facebook.com/melstringerart
**Tumblr:** http://melstringer.tumblr.com

## VICKY TRAINOR, *UK*
## BRAND: THE LINEN GARDEN & THE VINTAGE DRAWER

**Website:** http://www.thevintagedrawer.com
**Website/shop:** www.thelinengarden.co.uk
**Blog:** www.thelinengarden.blogspot.com
**Etsy:** http://www.etsy.com/shop/vickytrainor
**Facebook Page:** www.facebook.com/VickyTrainorStationery
**Twitter:** https://twitter.com/vickytrainor
**Bloglovin':** http://www.bloglovin.com/blog/4409169/the-linen-garden

## AMANDA WRIGHT, *USA*
## BRAND: WIT & WHISTLE

**Website:** http://witandwhistle.com
**Blog:** http://witandwhistle.com/blog
**Etsy:** http://www.etsy.com/shop/witandwhistle
**Shop:** http://witandwhistle.com/shop
**Facebook Page:** www.facebook/witandwhistle
**Twitter:** https://twitter.com/witandwhistle
**Pinterest:** http://pinterest.com/witandwhistle

# INDEX

Page numbers in *italics* refer to photographs.

# ABOUT THE AUTHOR

From an early age, Torie Jayne fell in love with all aspects of design. After focusing on fashion while studying at Kingston University in London, her first job was in New York designing for American Eagle Outfitters. Returning to London, she continued her fifteen-year career, working for many High Street brands, such as Marks & Spencer and Zara, designing collections in many areas, from swimwear and knitwear, to denim and childrenswear.

Upon buying her first home, Torie's passion for crafts and interiors was given free rein, as she took on house beautification projects with her eye for colour combinations and attention to detail. In 2010 she started her blog, http://toriejayne.blogspot.co.uk/, as a means of sharing her baking, crafting and interior design ideas with others. In combination with her Pinterest boards (pinterest.com/toriejayne) and Flickr photo stream (flickr.com/photos/toriejayne), Torie has demonstrated exceptional skills with colour and trend awareness, and has built an online brand that attracts around 100,000 hits a month to her blog alone.

The experience of living and working in the US, in combination with extensive worldwide travel throughout her career, has ensured her inspiration and trend awareness is truly international. Although Torie's blog is UK-based, the readership is multinational, with more than a third of the audience being American.

Her passion for decorating for seasonal holidays is evident on her blog, which features many different crafts, including handmade cake stands, embroidered tablecloths, glittered toadstools, needle-felted acorns and snowflake placemats. Her dessert table tableaux proved incredibly popular, containing the prettiest macarons, quirkiest cake pops, extravagantly decorated cakes, gingerbread bird houses, iced doughnuts, sweet and chocolate bunny lollipops, complete with hand-designed and manufactured gift wrap labels and packaging.

Birds feature heavily in her work, from polka-dot fabric Easter birds to black crows at Halloween and a birdcage Christmas cake, as well as numerous hanging bird decorations.

Torie's creative work on her blog has appeared in global publications, including *The Magic of Sugar* in Germany, *Making* magazine in the UK, the Dutch magazine *Ariadne at Home*, the French magazine *C'est dit!*, ACP magazines in Australia, Arnoldo Mondadori publications in Italy, and *Cosmopolitan Greece*. Online publications have also published her work, including *Apartment Therapy, Mollie Makes, Creature Comforts, Be Different...Act Normal* and *Heart Home*.

Having built a successful online brand for Torie Jayne, Torie now wishes to focus full-time on her crafting and baking passions and is working with her childhood sweetheart, an IT developer, to turn her blog into a website with integrated video tutorials as well as an iPad app.

## ACKNOWLEDGEMENTS

It is with much joy and happiness that I get to thank all the people that made this dream a reality. So a big, warm, heartfelt thank you goes to: Sussie Bell for her beautiful photography, fun-filled trips and wonderful support. Vicky, Emma, Elyse, Helena, Tamar, Tabitha, Mel, Jamie, Carmen, Nellianna, Kenneth, Fleur, Whitney, Annabelle, Amanda and Anne for all of their fabulous contributions. Sonya for finding me and Caroline for all her great work. My Mum and Dad for encouraging me to pursue my dreams. My family and friends for support, laughter and understanding. My Torie Jayne readers and blogging friends who light up my life. George for being my number one fan, and last but by no means least, to my amazing Keiran whose unwavering daily support, love and encouragement has made this possible.

## CREDITS

Craft desk project laser-cut panels by Budget Signs, Chingford, UK and spray paint from PlastiKote®.

Photography of individual crafters and their products supplied by themselves. Elyse Major's photographs were taken by Marisa Bettencourt and Emma Lamb's craft space by Sussie Bell.

Corbis Images, page 133
GAP Interior Images Ltd, pages 2–3, 62–3

All other photographs were taken by Sussie Bell and are copyright of Quintet Publishing Ltd. Craft fair photographs were taken at Selina Lake's Handmade & Vintage Summer Fete, Kingston upon Thames, UK.

Ribbons for ribbon spool holder project from Jane Means.